# Monarchies

# Monarchies

## Demos Collection / issue 17

**Editors**
Tom Bentley
James Wilsdon

**Production editor**
Eddie Gibb

Cover design by The Set Up, London
Typeset by Politico's Design, London
Printed by Biddles Ltd, Guildford

Demos Collection is
published twice a year by
Demos
Elizabeth House
39 York Road
London
SE1 7NQ

tel: 020 7401 5330
fax: 020 7401 5331

mail@demos.co.uk
www.demos.co.uk

ISBN 1 84180 039 2

**Demos** is an independent think tank
committed to radical thinking on the
long-term problems facing the UK
and other advanced industrial
societies.

It aims to develop ideas – both theo-
retical and practical – to help shape
the politics of the twenty-first century,
and to improve the breadth and
quality of political debate.

Demos publishes books and a
regular journal, and undertakes substantial empirical and policy oriented
research projects. Demos is a
registered charity.

NESTA (The National Endowment for
Science, Technology and the Arts)
encourages leading edge, creative
thinking and new ideas and is
delighted to promote talent in the
field of essay writing.
www.nesta.org.uk

# Contents

Monarchies: what are kings and queens for?

## Acknowledgements

Many thanks to all our contributors, and to the entire Demos team for help at various stages of this project. Particular thanks to Jules Margo, for her invaluable contribution at the commissioning stage, and to Eddie Gibb for masterminding the editing and production process.

Tim Hames and Mark Leonard deserve a special mention, as their 1998 Demos pamphlet *Modernising the Monarchy* provided the firm foundations on which this collection could build.

Finally, we are grateful to NESTA (The National Endowment for Science, Technology and the Arts) for their generous support of the project.

**Tom Bentley and James Wilsdon**
May 2002

# Part 1

## God save the Queen?

# The new monarchists

Can a class-bound institution turn itself into
a progressive family which leads the nation?

**Tom Bentley and James Wilsdon**

*'Change has become a constant; managing it has become an
expanding discipline.'* HM Queen Elizabeth II, 30 April 2002

After a decade dominated by divorce, scandal and tragedy, the
British royals are once again riding high on a wave of public
and media adulation. The Golden Jubilee, written off in
advance as the biggest damp squib since the Millennium
Dome, looks set to be a roaring success. Opinion polls are reg-
istering support for the monarchy at their highest levels for
years. As Jonathan Freedland admitted recently, 'these are days
for republicans to walk humbly'.[1]

It wasn't meant to be like this. Conventional wisdom had it
that the monarchy faced gentle but inevitable decline; a fragile
anachronism unable to resist the forces of modernity which
are undermining all sources of traditional authority. Assisted
by the boorish behaviour of the younger Windsors, the
monarchy should have tottered into the twenty first century,
then keeled over and given up, or at the very least consigned
itself to bicycling irrelevance.

But despite two major bereavements this year, the monarchy
has a new spring in its step. A decade on from the Queen's
*annus horribilis*, 2002 looks set to become an *annus mirabilis*.

1 Freedland, J. (2002)
'The story of us, not
them', *The Guardian*, 12
April

For the first time since the mid-1980s, the royal stock is rising and the institution is back in fashion.

Several factors have contributed to this revival. Firstly, the programme of incremental reforms initiated in the early 1990s and accelerated in the wake of Diana's death, has helped to neutralise some public disquiet. Under the watchful eyes of the Palace's Way Ahead Group, the Queen has started paying taxes; Buckingham Palace was opened to the public; the civil list has been slimmed and opened to greater Parliamentary scrutiny; and the royal yacht has been decommissioned. These reforms helped disarm the 'civil list republicans' who have attacked royal wealth. There is now a widespread sense that the royal family offers greater value for money, so that the successful avoidance of death duties this year has raised barely a murmur. As Evan Davis puts it in this collection, for an annual cost per citizen of around 2p a week, we enjoy something 'far grander, far less commercial and more genuinely publicly owned than anything the private sector could provide'.

Second, the royal family has become highly adept in its use of PR and media management through the bought-in talents of experts such as Simon Walker and Mark Bolland. The delicate handling of Prince Harry's drug-taking, the fly-on-the-wall images of Prince William's gap year, the striking images of the Queen Mother's funeral and the skilful choreography of the Queen's Jubilee Tour displayed a deft PR touch. The drama of recent events enhanced ongoing efforts to soften the royal family's image, including the Queen's occasional forays into pubs and Prince Charles's encounter with the Spice Girls. The combined effect is of a monarchy far more closely in touch with the lifestyles and concerns of its subjects.

Third, there are almost inevitable peaks and troughs in the royal narrative in Britain's cultural and political life. Public support for the institution wavered several times in the last century, most recently after Diana's death, when the ferocity of the backlash forced the Queen to make an unscheduled address to the nation.[2] Until this year, the royal family had struggled to recover the popularity it lost in the 1990s; an ICM poll in 2001 found support for a republic at an all time high of 34 per cent.

Yet as John Yorke points out in his essay, there is nothing we

2 For a detailed history of republicanism see Prochaska, F. (2000) The Republic of Britain 1760-2000 Penguin, London

like more than seeing triumph snatched from the jaws of defeat. Redemption is one of the core motifs of all great narratives, from Shakespeare to soap opera, and one to which we are all emotionally attuned. That a Jubilee – which literally means a season for rejoicing – should immediately follow a time of mourning has a symbolic resonance deep within our culture. However subconsciously, there is a sense that the Queen Mother's death has atoned for the 'sins' of the past decade.

A final reason for renewed royal confidence is the loss of momentum in New Labour's constitutional reform programme. Lord Jenkins' report on electoral reform gathers dust, while the stalled reform of the House of Lords provides a lesson in the dangers of taking a sledgehammer to our institutional architecture without a clear vision for its replacement. English devolution is being delivered in a non-committal way. New Labour's talk of a 'young country' has been replaced by a managerial focus on public services. In Scotland, Wales, and London we see the mechanics of devolution but little passion for revitalising democracy. While concern about voter disaffection has become mainstream among politicians, it has not yet matured into a coherent view on how constitutional reform might reinvigorate democracy.

Veiled threats that monarchists might have glimpsed in New Labour's initial burst of modernisation have proved baseless. Any sense that New Labour had the energy, legitimacy or vision to challenge the Windsors' established position is clearly gone. This pragmatic government is far more interested in delivering on policy than in rethinking fundamental democratic structures. Like most Prime Ministers before him, Tony Blair appears to have grown genuinely fond of the Queen. And as Vernon Bogdanor has observed, the monarchy 'offers fixed constitutional landmarks and a degree of institutional continuity in a changing world, so that the costs of change [to society] come to appear easier to bear'.[3] Following Gladstone, Asquith, Attlee and Wilson, Blair has conformed to the rule that progressive Prime Ministers make the staunchest royalists.

### Modernisation revisited?

Attempts to consolidate support for the monarchy seem to be pushing at an open door. However, none of this means that

**3** Bogdanor, V. (1995) *The Monarchy and the Constitution*, Oxford University Press

more fundamental reform is off the agenda. Media mastery and incremental change can provide short bursts of public support, but as New Labour itself has discovered, they cannot indefinitely avoid more searching questions about the kind of society we live in, and the suitability of our public institutions. And while the Queen Mother's death cued up the successful presentation of a unified, re-legitimised monarchy in 2002, it will also mark the opening up of a new generation of challenges for the Windsors.

The Queen Mother's passing marked the end of a period during which the contribution of Elizabeth II's rule was unquestioned. The pattern was set by the 1936 abdication crisis and subsequent wartime experience, followed by a half century in which the Queen sought to exemplify those values and duties which she clearly sees as central to the British character. The most pressing question, though, is not whether she has performed those duties with integrity, but whether her reign has enabled the monarchy to adapt successfully to a new century.

Four years ago, in the Demos pamphlet *Modernising the Monarchy*, Tim Hames and Mark Leonard moved beyond the sterile confrontation between republicans and monarchists by offering a blueprint for a more accountable and democratic monarchy.[4] They argued that a clear majority of the British public support its continued existence, but would prefer the institution to be modernised. Their arguments are now being taken up by others. As Frank Prochaska has argued, the great weakness of republicanism has been its failure to consider any explanation for monarchy's continued existence 'beyond tradition, mass delusion or plutocratic convenience'.[5] The main purpose of this collection is further to deepen our understanding of a monarchy's relevance in the UK and beyond.

As Jonathan Parry argues, the importance of adapting to changing times is not new to the British monarchy; its endurance is based partly on its ability to present a 'representative' face to its people over at least the last 200 years. Richard Webb suggests that there are even deeper roots in human nature which may support, or at least explain, our willingness to accept divisions of social status organised around a figure of ultimate authority. Such systems operate across the social world of

**4** Hames, T. & Leonard, M. (1998) *Modernising the Monarchy*, Demos, London
**5** Prochaska, F., op cit, p.223

animals, and have particular value for humans in helping to prevent perpetual conflict within the group. The historical role of chiefs in structuring and protecting group identity is relatively clear. The hereditary principle which makes transition peaceful and uncontroversial has a similar logic, although history suggests that there are relatively few periods when monarchical succession has achieved these qualities.

But the central question is how monarchies can retain their purpose when the central function for which they evolved – ruling – has been made obsolete. As Ken Gladdish makes clear, the surviving European monarchies are historical exceptions, following two clear periods of state-making. New nineteenth century nations took it for granted that emulating the great powers of the time required full royal regalia. Following the First World War, however, aspiring twentieth century nations were more likely to look to presidential republics like the USA.

The monarchies which survived both periods have avoided total regime collapse, as in Germany, and have willingly ceded their political powers to other institutions, as in Sweden and Denmark. The British monarchy is a peculiarity, in that it suffered its most serious crisis between the world wars (the 1936 abdication), relegitimised itself by identifying with its public during the struggle against Nazism, and has since relinquished virtually none of its wealth, status or prerogative powers.

### The imperfections of politicians

One important part of the monarchists' defence is to cast doubt on the value of the alternatives. Public disdain for professional politicians means that proposing an elected head of state as an automatically superior option seems weak. As Matt Peacock makes clear, the perceived inadequacy of the proposed alternative in the recent Australian referendum did as much to secure the Queen's victory as any respect or affection Australians might feel for her. There are some good arguments for making the head of state a figure above party politics, and for retaining an efficient method of succession.

Yet this argument does not square with the prerogative powers to intervene directly in political decisions which our Queen still holds. The public is largely unaware of these powers, but their occasional use usually leads to a challenge, as in the case of King Baudouin of Belgium's relatively recent refusal as a Catholic to sign an abortion bill. When the Governor General intervened to dismiss an elected government during the Australian constitutional crisis of 1975, the Queen's role was shown to be more than symbolic.

Nobody exemplifies this tension better than Prince Charles. His various passions have occupied him while distracting the rest of the society from the vacuous role of the monarch-in-waiting. There is no doubt that the Prince's Trust and some of his other initiatives have been socially constructive, but it is very difficult to imagine the public tolerating a king who is as personally motivated. And it is equally difficult to imagine a monarch in his 50s or 60s who can suddenly learn the habits of impartiality while engaging daily in affairs of state.

This collection also throws up a surprisingly consistent set of themes around which monarchy might secure future public legitimacy: celebrity, and the status of royals as stars in a media-dominated, personality-obsessed era; public service and commitment to the needs of whole societies, including the disadvantaged; and the heritage value of palaces and castles with living occupants. But the real question is whether our monarchy has the resources to balance the tension between these new roles and its own past.

How credible, for example, can a commitment to the poor be from a family who assiduously protect huge personal wealth, and whose retinues reinforce rank and formal status? Can diversity, tolerance and respect be championed by people holding titles which still reflect the imperial conquest by Britain of much of the rest of the world? Will royals steeped in centuries-old traditions of social etiquette survive in the melee of twenty first century society? Could King Charles promote interfaith understanding while acting as Supreme Governor and Defender of the Faith? The sight of royal family members shuttling between palaces at a time when the number of households in the UK exceeds the available dwellings should alarm even die-hard monarchists.

Further slimming of the civil list, and periodic review of the costs of the royal household might well be useful, but running costs are not the core issue, as Evan Davis argues. The bigger question is whether this intensely hierarchical staff structure that the civil list supports can respond to the changing needs of a more diverse and less deferential public. Or do they by definition represent a much narrower, class-based set of interests which are incapable of adapting to Britain's changing sense of identity?

There is little sense that the surface-level, PR-driven reforms of recent years will be sufficient to meet these long-term challenges. Indeed, the more the monarchy lives by the rules of the media, the more likely it is to end up suffering at their hands. As Chris Rojek argues, the consequence of the royals joining David Beckham, Robbie Williams and Kate Winslet in the pantheon of modern celebrity is that they are subjected to the same levels of scrutiny. This is fine if you are a pop idol or an *EastEnders* star who can survive the glare of the tabloids for two years and then retire on the proceeds. But a lifetime in the public gaze – the 60-year ordeal which William and Harry now face – is profoundly unsustainable. Princess Diana thrived in this arena, but as a result clashed spectacularly and destructively with the hidden power of the Windsors.

The danger, as Mary Riddell makes clear, is that the continuation of monarchy by traditional means increases a 'stuckness' in British society. There is a dependence on nostalgia and a sense of identity which has become too fragile to accommodate the tensions within Britain. The strategy of incremental change by the Royals now looks dangerous, with an increasing risk of scandal or sudden loss of public support.

## A post-modern monarchy

The Queen recently mused on the constancy of change, but added: 'I would like above all to declare my resolve to continue.' The royal redemption strategy now relies on a timeless and dutiful counterpoint to the diversity and disorientation of modern life. The Queen aims to provide symbolic unity and tireless service which represents the whole of the UK in a way that no other institution could hope to do.

This will be well received, especially in Jubilee year. But its relevance to non-deferential younger generations, which lack the war-time experience which seems crucial to cementing public affection, is marginal. Even now, most polls show a solid 30 per cent in favour of radical reform.[6] When the current surge in popularity inevitably subsides, the need for a long-term strategy of institutional renewal will be as pressing as ever.

Yet it is equally clear that the impetus for reform will not come from without. Politicians do not have the incentive, or the public support, to force the pace of change. Institutions which thrive over time are those most capable of adapting to changed circumstances. Increasingly, such adaptation is understood in evolutionary terms.[7] Evolutionary change does not have to be glacial; in fact, to avoid extinction, rapid bursts of learning and adaptation are sometimes required.

The outlines of an agenda for creating a sustainable post-modern monarchy are partly familiar, partly new.

It would start with an explicit acknowledgment that the monarchy's primary function is now symbolic rather than con-stitutional. Few people are aware of the monarchy's formal powers or enthusiastic about retaining them, but the symbolic role could be usefully strengthened. We need a cultural rather than a constitutional monarchy which can contribute to wider democratic renewal.

This means retaining the monarch as head of state but severing direct connections to executive, parliament and judiciary. As Graham Allen argues, this task could be accompanied by codifying and limiting the powers of the Prime Minister. The task of unified representation of a diverse nation also implies that the monarch should not exclusively represent a single religious insti-tution, a move which would arguably free the Church of England to develop its own much-needed strategy for renewal.[8]

This kind of constitutional reform would not in itself make the UK a more democratic society. But the reserves of influence that the royal family holds over the workings of the constitu-tion act as the democratic equivalent of treacle, slowing the potential for change rather than lubricating a venerable system. The longer term challenge of developing the tech-niques, cultures and constitutional structures needed to ensure a vibrant democracy requires urgent attention, but is a separate task.

6 Independent/ICM poll, 9 April 2002
7 Bentley, T, 'Letting go: complexity, individualism and the left', Renewal, Spring 2002
8 For details of how the Monarchy could be dis-entangled from the workings of the state, see for example Modernising the Monarchy pp.21-34; or Richards, P. (1996) Long to Reign over us? Fabian Society, London

Other elements of a renewal programme could include new forms of access to the public space offered by royal parks and properties, symbolised by opening up Buckingham Palace Gardens and the surrounding parks to new forms of use, as Terry Farrell proposes. A wider review of crown land which sought to ease housing pressure and improve public access could also flow from such a move, with the royal family vacating a number of properties.

Overhauling the honours system and reviewing the charitable involvement of the royal family to reflect a wider range of social priorities would also fit this pattern, as would changing the way in which younger royals are trained for their roles. One option might be to send them to state schools. This would send a powerful democratising signal through our education system and effectively remove the 'by royal appointment' stamp which maintains the privileged position of the elite public schools. As a result, future princes and princesses would be far better prepared for a life of service to the whole of British society.

Another crucially important area, in which Charles has already shown interest, lies in helping to nurture and reflect the nation's spiritual needs, through promoting interfaith education and exploring newer forms of spiritual expression.

Similarly, Britain's traditional connections with the rest of the world provide an opportunity to reinvent the role of the Commonwealth and forge new approaches to reconciliation, conflict prevention and poverty reduction. This could begin with a world tour which apologised for Imperial wrongs, combined with a new effort to make the Commonwealth effective and relevant to the new challenges of globalisation. These measures would help to transform perceptions of both the UK and its monarchy.

**Quit while you're ahead, Ma'am**
Reinvention is unlikely to occur under an institutional head who has presided for half a century. This is surely an appropriate moment to ask whether the Queen is the right person to lead the next phase. Recent speeches suggest that she recognises the scale of the challenge, but her rhetoric belies a record of reactive, rather than proactive, reform. This is nowhere

more visible than in her failure to create a successful model for her own succession.

The 1936 abdication crisis is likely to have had a deep impact on the psychology of the Queen and her generation. But just at the moment when a new stage of debate should be opened, the Queen has attempted to silence it.

At 76, there is something absurd about anyone declaring their intention to keep going forever. When Elizabeth came to the throne in 1952, the average life expectancy for women was 71 years. In 2002, this has risen to 80.[9] If the Queen lives as long as her mother, her reign could extend for another 25 years. But just imagine the scenario of her next Jubilee: in June 2027, the Queen is 101, Charles is 79 and William is 45. Monarchy is in danger of being replaced by gerontocracy.

The average age of a FTSE 100 chief executive is 51 and has fallen by ten years since 1990[10]. Charles is now 53 and as ready as he will ever be to run the family firm. The Queen should acknowledge this, and use the Jubilee year to set out a clear strategy for the succession. A sensible option would be to announce that she intends to hand over to Charles on her 80th birthday in 2006. By then, William would have had two years of post-graduate experience and would be ready to assume the responsibilities of heir.

Some argue that the answer is to skip a generation, bypassing Charles III for William V. This might become inevitable, but would be a far bigger risk. Nothing can insulate the succession from the risks of instability; only experimentation with a new style will establish whether it can be successful.

In a self-governing society, there is ultimately no justification for forms of wealth and privilege which have their roots in the deference and authority of the past. The depth of the social and cultural changes we are undergoing is unlikely to slow over the next half century – it will bring new strains and contradictions to British society. Whether the British monarchy remains to help resolve them will depend on imagination and bravery, as well as on its sense of public duty.

*Tom Bentley is the director of Demos, and James Wilsdon is head of strategy.*

**9** Government Actuary's Department, Office for National Statistics
**10** Pye, A, (2000) 'Changing scenes in, from and outside the boardroom', *Corporate Governance*

# By popular acclaim

Why the monarchy must make sacrifices for
a more equal Britain

**Mary Riddell**

Meeting royalty has a Godot factor. At any event attended by a
member of the royal family, the invitees must be in place long
before the honoured guest arrives. Security is an issue,
naturally. Prince Charles has been approached by an eccentric
with a fake weapon, and the late Queen Mother once smashed
her lace-trimmed parasol over the head of a man following her
carriage, unaware that he wanted to give her daughter a ten-
shilling note. But excessive waiting also has a deeper purpose.

When eventually the royal visitor enters, the squashed
hordes will be hotter and humbler, constrained by new
clothes, tight shoes and an unexpected awe of a representative
of a family that knows how to command a deference out of
kilter with its popularity. A third of the population wants a
republic, a third couldn't care what befalls the monarchy, but
damp-palmed curtseyers abound. While this reverence may be
bogus and temporary, it still offers evidence that the House of
Windsor can deploy the mystique Walter Bagehot isolated as
the one essential ingredient of survival.

Arguably, the reservoir of fake fealty has deepened, rather
than diminished, as the Windsors' popularity has slumped.
The idle aristocracy that used to offer camaraderie rather than
deference is busy selling stately home marmalade to stave off

death duties and dry rot. The working classes of the East End, dismissed by Victoria's attendant as 'socialists and the worst Irish' when they booed the Queen, are less feral. The British class structure, so compartmentalised in 1950 that 95 per cent of the population knew which socioeconomic box they ticked, is amorphous now.

### Between deference and derision

Sycophants and hecklers have lost some of their sway, leaving an extended middle class to work out its conflicting response to modern royalty. Difficult divorces, toe-kissing financial advisers, tea parties with fake sheikhs, cannabis scandals, under-age drinking binges and Weight Watchers endorsements have made the Windsors, with some exceptions, objects of derision. So why, in an egalitarian and critical age, should they also still command obeisance?

Partly because the flipside of scorn is pity. Only the harshest would not feel sorrow for a Queen whose sister and mother died within seven weeks of one another. But people feel sorry even for those royals least able to command respect. The Earl and Countess of Wessex are deemed too risible for serious criticism, while those who earn a 'most-loved' citation get placed almost beyond reproach. Before and after her death, the Queen Mother was regarded, by the edict of traditionalists, as a sweet and self-sacrificing martyr to duty.

She was also an indulged autocrat with a Rabelaisian appetite for luxury, a multimillion overdraft and high-Tory sympathies. Widowed young, she was at first mortified at having to relinquish power to her daughter. The £643,000 a year supplied by the taxpayer was her lifelong state compensation. Icon or cling-on? Such debate became almost treasonable in the days after her death. Nor was there much to learn from the battle between those in the right-wing press who vilified a supposedly Jacobin BBC and those who detected, in a few frustrated *Casualty* watchers demanding less royal coverage, the chrysalis of a republic. But neither did the many thousands who trooped past Her Majesty's coffin vindicate the loyalists' claim that reverence for old-style royalty is as fierce as ever.

Citizens who queued for 14 hours to see the catafalque – and the half a million who came to Westminster to watch the funeral – were engaged in something more complex than a simple act of allegiance to a beloved Queen Empress. They wanted to be participators in the news, rather than mere observers. They were keen to find, in a friendly crowd sharing tea and sandwiches, a communitarian spirit that politicians laud but cannot instil. They were also, inadvertently, underlining the fact that heritage worship is practised not by those societies most certain about who they are but by those least sure of their national identity.

Among the vast majority of people who stayed away, many also watched the televised funeral with awe. For some, it may have been a moving experience. For others, it will have offered a spectacle as gripping but emotionless as the Chinese State Circus. Both reactions are consistent with puzzlement, or anger, over a country better at window-dressing than content. When trains don't run on time, when motorways are clogged, when tradition decrees that we're scared to join the euro but we dare attack Iraq, when there is a famine of teachers, then Britain's status as the world's most lavish undertaker looks hollow.

But the best case for a reformed monarchy was made, ironically, not by the cynical but by loyal mourners. Some who queued through a cold night for a glimpse of the royal coffin were told just after dawn that Black Rod had closed Westminster Hall for two hours without explanation or notice. Throughout, ordinary people were allotted a walk-on role in a story redolent of old class values and featuring gracious royalty and loyal retainers, epitomised by 'Backstairs Billy', the Queen Mother's manservant. Although younger members of the royal family played the populist card (The Queen Mum was an Ali G fan. Respec!), something had altered. For the first time pageantry was questioned by those who detected, beyond vibrant heritage, a playschool country defined by its dressing-up box.

## The limits of republicanism
So what now? When faith in God wears thin and trust in politicians sinks lower, the monarchy can at least market itself as a

model of stolid continuum. Republicanism has thrown up few more enticing avatars than Cromwell and President Hattersley. Despite flutters of public enthusiasm, nothing much has changed since the years before Queen Victoria's birth. When all of George III's 56 other grandchildren were illegitimate and the Hanoverian line looked doomed, there were strong hopes among liberal progressives that the hereditary monarchy was over and that Britain would follow the example of the United States.

Today, President Bush's America, complete with Enron, the death penalty and hawkish foreign policy, looks rather less like the paradigm of fairness and entitlement that the architects of the constitution envisaged. Besides, the most powerful supporter of the British status quo is America, whose tourists marvel at the ceremonial palaces that serve a family costing more than all the other royal houses of Europe put together. So long as Britons believe that national identity and economic buoyancy are enmeshed with the survival of an overblown House of Windsor, Her Majesty's subjects collude in promoting the monarchy's folklore as their own.

One myth that the royal family has successfully peddled, with the help of Tony Blair, is that the Windsors are late converts to populism. The notion of Diana as a 'people's princess' ignored the fact that the 'common touch' is chiefly practised by those royals who are most adept at creating the illusion that monarchy exists for the benefit of ordinary folk. There is, as yet, almost no evidence that the royal family (while possibly willing to jettison some of its minor players) has any urge to amend its own lifestyle.

The signs are, conversely, that the Queen and Prince Charles would be much more pragmatic about shedding the unwarranted political power wielded by a constitutional monarch. If there is enough demand, the Queen may amend the Act of Settlement, which forbids a Catholic from taking the throne. Primogeniture is unlikely to be insisted on for much longer. Disestablishment of the Church of England, endorsed by some bishops, may suit a future king who sees himself as a 'defender of faith' and who wants to marry his mistress.

The truly sacrosanct areas, for an apolitical Queen and her highly political heir alike, are wealth and status. Minor gestures apart, both are non-negotiable. Blue-blooded courtiers may get replaced by a secondee from British Gas or a plumber's son. The Queen might visit McDonald's, sign a football, dispense with the Royal Yacht and pay (in contravention of her late mother's wishes) a nominal amount in tax. She might iron old Christmas wrapping paper, save bits of string and stick to one bar on the electric fire. Such frugalities, reminiscent of her mother's habit of having Highland Spring bottles filled with tap water, signal only an intention to cling on to all assets, small or great.

## Charles III: the people's king?

Prince Charles, similarly, has some ascetic tastes. His Prince's Trust demonstrates a constructive approach to poverty and deprivation that Diana, despite her crowd-pleasing charity work, never came close to emulating. Whether devising kitsch townships or producing not-for-profit shortbread biscuits, Charles can demonstrate a more or less sure social conscience. The state of the nation – its poverty, its prisons, its Wimpey architecture and its frail ecostructure – preys on his mind. And yet it seems far from certain that the Prince, while happy to axe some fringe royals, would use his accession to concede a single palace or privilege. In his view, the British public yearns for continuity and tradition; something, as he once put it to me, that 'isn't frenetically fashionable but is just there'.

Any reduction in lackeys or ceremonial would, under that argument, chip away at the nation's lust for cosy certainties. The Prince of Wales is not a greedy man, simply an aspiring monarch for whom personal wealth and status correlate conveniently with the public good. In a democratic society, does this dubious assumption matter? For two reasons, it does. The first is that an obsession with tradition and the plastic Beefeater branch of history is a brake on Britain as a modern nation. We risk becoming the dowager of Europe, peering at the progress of others through a lorgnette of nostalgia and heritage. Behind the Chancellor's five economic tests for joining the euro lies the insularity of a country schooled by its traditions of monarchy always to look back and never forward.

The broader problem of a royal family at the apex of an

anachronistic class structure is that such status is not simply symbolic. It reinforces the unfairness of a society that thinks itself more equal than it is. The glacial one-upmanship of Evelyn Waugh and Anthony Powell may have vanished or been muted, but Oxbridge places still go to the wealthiest few, and social mobility is less fluid than the new, catch-all middle class structure suggests. Even the Labour Party hierarchy still favours top drawer contenders, rather than more proletarian candidates. As DJ Taylor pointed out recently in the *New Statesman*, the party always picks its ideologues and leaders – Attlee, Crosland and now Blair – from the expensively educated bourgeoisie, rather than the working class.

## A nation ill at ease with itself

The recent attack by Gavyn Davies, the chairman of the BBC, on the corporation's mockers as 'white, middle-aged and middle-class', prompted two reactions. One was a defence of the white middle classes by the white middle classes. The second was a suggestion that Mr Davies, elevated by his wealth to the pluto-cratic upper stratum that has moved in to fill a Wooster-shaped vacuum, was simply being snobbish. More probably, he was expressing frustration. The BBC, though clever at identifying a young, multiracial, diverse audience living north of Hampstead, cannot work out how to reach or charm it.

Old institutions – the monarchy, the church and the public service broadcaster alike – seem powerless to bridge a cultural gulf. Neither the royal creed of *noblesse oblige* nor New Labour's mantra of meritocracy resonate in a Britain where black, Asian and other British-born minorities are more than 7 per cent of a 57 million population. Yet we are still the subjects of hunting, shooting, fishing monarchs whose own multicul-tural past, from imperial Russia to Hanover, was long since homogenised into upper-class Britishness.

The disjunction between the House of Windsor and the society over which it presides was marked out as insupportable in the days after the Queen Mother died. Despite the crowds and tears, the 'mourn-or-else' clamour of the right wing crys-tallised unease in the majority population. As the Queen Mother lay in state, they were burying other grandmothers in

Bethlehem. MPs called back to Parliament for an emergency session of eulogies were not permitted to discuss the crisis in the Middle East.

Perhaps the Queen Mother's funeral was the hour at which the monarchy drew closest to its most loyal subjects. It was also a reminder of the gap between the top and the bottom of society. Crowded prisons, a rise in violent crime, struggling schools, pregnant teenagers and hard-drinking children cannot be branded, like the words 'By Royal Appointment' on a pickle jar, as the especial product of the House of Windsor. In any case, social superiority, *pace* Prince Harry's exploits, is no insurance against yobbishness. But equally, the hereditary principle is not simply a Jobcentre for kings or queens. Trickle-down privilege means that outcomes for too many citizens are determined by accident of birth.

## Class and the hereditary principle

In March 2002, the Royal Economic Society produced evidence that Britain is becoming a less socially mobile society.[1] Those who are born at the top of the heap are likely to stay there, and vice versa. The wealthiest monopolise the best education and the best-paid jobs, while children from poorer families who grew up in the 1980s found it harder than their equivalents of the two preceding decades to get a better job and a higher salary than their parents.

The working class has got smaller as manual jobs declined, but the new recruits to the middle class have not displaced the children of richer parents. The latter, however deficient in intellect or ambition, seem ring-fenced not by nepotism but by the fact that affluence offers automatic insurance against failure. Emphasis on universally high standards at school and an opening up of higher education suggest a new equality and an open-to-all society. Yet the social gap has widened. Thirty-five per cent of graduate farmers and 20 per cent of health professionals are doing the same job as their fathers. Less than 10 per cent of children move from the lowest to the highest social groups.

This unequal system, more pronounced than in almost any other developed country, defies both old socialist dreams of

1 Royal Economic Society, *Changes in Intergenerational Mobility in Britain* (London, 2002).

equality and New Labour's message that talent is the passport to success. Only the hereditary principle offers a reliable model for the way society works: a top-down structure in which monarchs and road-sweepers can ascribe their destiny to birthright.

While it would be absurd to blame the monarchy for all inequalities, it is self-evident that a society that demands excessive veneration and wealth for its top echelon offers a diminishing scale of kudos and bounty to the lesser ranks. The same goes for respect. It is insulting that citizens who can talk to politicians without ceremony must assume a pantomime obeisance in addressing a minor royal. In an informal age, modern Britain, with its creaky ceremonial, its swan-upping, guard-changing and state opening of Parliament, less resembles an evolving nation than a revival of *HMS Pinafore*.

In 1897, the medical statistician Arthur Newsholme recorded an infant mortality rate of 127 babies in every 1,000 live births in Hampstead, rising to 197 in the East End. Almost half of the working class lived in poverty and a 1900 Conference of Ladies on Domestic Hygiene was told of 'case after case of little match box makers working habitually from the time that school closes until 11pm'. Yet when the Queen Mother died, the century through which she had lived was painted almost universally as a balmy, blessed age.

And even now, one in four children remains poor. Although society has changed, a Victorian class system has blocked progress and threatens to impede it further. In a post-imperial age, Britain remains semi-detached from a changing Europe. The House of Lords has altered, the Human Rights Act is in place, but tradition, embodied in an unreformed monarchy, continues to stifle us. Change is long overdue, but the more strident voice belongs to fearful traditionalists.

### The slow path to modernisation

By contrast, the liberal progressive case is tentative. Wishful republicans dream of the revolution but never explain how a tenacious House of Windsor is to be dislodged. Modernisers call for more modest change: a monarchy that lives in the same world as the rest of us, that pays its taxes and relinquishes the royal prerogative.

A prime minister and government who find the monarchy a useful and harmless source of executive power are increasingly out of touch with the country's mood. The idea that a lapse from pristine family values has thrown the royal family into disrepute is nonsense. The late Queen Mother's most powerful brothers-in-law comprised an abdicator with a divorced mistress and a drug user of uncertain sexual orientation. The mystique of royalty has been dented not by the knowledge that they are too much like us but by the worry that they are not similar enough.

The move towards a slimmed-down monarchy more eager to pay its own way and to live less grandly should begin now. How, when empire has gone, the Commonwealth is in turmoil, and the House of Windsor gives little impression of serving any cause bar its own, does it propose to promote a modern Britain? Supplying the answer will not only involve constitutional pragmatism or crowd-pleasing gestures. It will also mean personal sacrifice. Without that, the monarchy will remain an emblem of the inequality that increasingly corrodes the nation.

In Marie Antoinette's France, or the Romanovs' Russia, such divergence proved catastrophic. In middle-class Britain, where even cynics thrill to an invitation from the Master of the Household, no such grim outcomes threaten. Nonetheless, there are few good long-term prospects for a monarchy that exploits its subjects' earnings, patience, credibility and goodwill. The Windsors' reverence for history and tradition makes it both ideally placed to read those warning signs and wholly unable to avert them.

That leaves citizens as the driver of a change that now looks inevitable. In the debate after the Queen Mother's death, the result depended not on the agenda of government, media or the royal family itself. Press coverage, coloured with the stridency of panic, proved that the public had moved beyond easy manipulation. Would the mood swing to mourning, indifference or hostility? It hardly mattered which. In a society where equality is illusory, people proved less divided and more powerful than they knew. The consensus of those who decry change in the monarchy and those who demand it was identical. Nothing will be the same again. There has rarely been a clearer mandate for reform.

*Mary Riddell is a columnist for the* Observer *and an interviewer for the* New Statesman *and the* Daily Mail.

# After deference

The future of the monarchy in a value-for-money age

**Ben Pimlott**

Does the British monarchy *have* a future? In some ways, the celebration of the Queen's Golden Jubilee may seem an odd moment to ask such a question. That it should nevertheless in other ways seem an appropriate and even pressing one is an indication of the revolution in attitudes that has occurred in the last generation. In royal terms, we live in interesting times. Elizabeth II's reign has seen an overturning of the traditional view of an institution which, for most of the time since the early years of the reign of Victoria, had been revered like no other.

When Elizabeth acceded to the throne in 1952, the monarchy was a focal point of national life. Although lacking in political power, its significance was much more than merely ceremonial. In turbulent decades, the monarch had stood for nation and empire, while the royal family provided reassurance, and received respect and admiration in due measure. Indeed, until the 1960s, the Lord Chamberlain forbade even the most obsequious representation of any recent king or queen on the stage, as if it were a kind of blasphemy.

Fifty years has seen the almost complete erosion of a state of mind that made open discussion of Britain's oldest institution virtually taboo. Starting with the criticisms of the court made by Lord Altrincham (later John Grigg) in 1957, and encouraged first by the Palace's own abandonment of reticence and then by a tabloid search for revelations, the last half-century witnessed an accelerating trend towards greater frankness and public awareness. A remnant of the old attitude remains: serious politicians still hold back from attacks on the monarchy. However, for more than a decade, there has been open season in the press on the topic of royalty. Meanwhile, republicanism has entered the mainstream of political debate, and is unlikely to leave it.

In retrospect, some kind of end-of-century change of climate was bound to come. Hastened by royal scandal and misjudgement, the new frankness reflected developments over which the dynasty had no control. Altered attitudes to hierarchy, democracy, accountability and equality had little to do with the Windsors, yet were bound to bring a hereditary institution under scrutiny. At the same time, press censorship and self-constraint could scarcely have survived the growth of globalised media that regarded all public or famous people as their quarry. Neither is the more permissive atmosphere necessarily bad for the institution in the long run. Doubtless there have been times when Buckingham Palace has felt a pang of nostalgia for the old days. In general, however, the modern court recognises the undesirability – as well as the impossibility – of cordoning off one section of the constitution and giving it special treatment.

## A gradual decline

Nevertheless, the effect has been traumatic, producing a crisis of public confidence that has been deeper and more long-lasting than at any time since the Regency period. Where will it end? In the early nineteenth century there was fear of revolution, but also the knowledge that most states were monarchical, and likely to remain so. In the twenty-first century, though constitutional monarchies continue to exist in Europe and Asia, there has been a gentle decline in their significance, and the trend is unlikely to be reversed. In Britain, pressure on the monarchy has abated, and the disappearance or even scaling down of the institution does not seem imminent. This does not mean, however, that radical change is not foreseeable.

According to most opinion polls, the monarchy means less and less to younger people, and the proportion of the population that believes that it will not exist in 50 years' time has grown significantly.

Other parts of the former British empire have already led the way. In addition to those former colonies that abandoned the monarchy at independence or shortly after it, a number of Commonwealth 'realms' in which the monarch was once revered have either reduced the role of the queen (as in Canada) to a purely titular headship, or teetered on the brink of full republicanism. The Australian example shows how quickly attitudes can change. A nation that was previously – if anything – even more royalist than Britain experienced a gradual decline in loyalty to the point at which the previously unimaginable became the central platform of a major political party. Although the 2000 referendum vote went decisively against a republic, most observers see this as a temporary reprieve. Meanwhile, as other countries increase in confidence and national self-awareness, it is reasonable to assume that support for the monarchy elsewhere in the Commonwealth will also diminish.

## Whose Commonwealth?

Indeed, some predict the effective demise of the 'Commonwealth monarchy' when the present Queen dies, or steps down. The Prince of Wales has shown notably less interest in the overseas realms than his mother. Much will depend on world and local conditions at the start of Charles's reign and the behaviour of second (and third) generation royals during the remainder of the present one. Then there is the question of the Commonwealth headship, which is not constitutionally hereditary, and hence does not automatically pass to the Queen's successor. There is also the separate question of the 'realms'. In some of these, politicians who baulk at deposing the present monarch may well seize the opportunity of a changeover to end what increasing numbers see as an anachronistic arrangement. If so, Commonwealth republicanism could well become a fast-spreading contagion.

The Commonwealth is one thing. Britain another. There is

no technical reason why the United Kingdom should not follow the example of other, decreasingly monarchical realms. Indeed, in Britain the transfer of head of state functions to an elected or appointed non-royal president, or to a designated post-holder such as the Speaker of the House of Commons, is not only theoretically possible but – if backed by a wide consensus – technically achievable within a short period of time. As yet, however, the consensus in Britain remains the other way. Some of the reasons for the decline of the monarchy abroad do not apply here – in particular, the argument that the British sovereign is 'foreign'. Furthermore, an institution which elsewhere can be seen as a colonial legacy has in this country an unquestionable antiquity, which makes it harder to disentangle from other ancient or traditional components of church and state.

There is also the point that while a transition to a republican system might technically be smooth, the political problems could become a nightmare. Here, the antipodean debacle is salutary. The Westminster Parliament could find it as difficult as its Canberra equivalent to resolve the question of who should appoint the non-hereditary head of state – the political elite, or the general public. Legally, the monarchy in the United Kingdom could be abolished by a simple Act of Parliament passed by both Houses, which (as Walter Bagehot foresaw more than a century ago) the monarch would have no constitutional option but to approve. But for such a thing to come about, there would have to be a widespread mood in favour of such a change, almost certainly involving a referendum. Even if the monarchy died, in effect, of public boredom, the political system could well be convulsed, as politicians woke up to the reality that a popularly-elected president might acquire a democratic legitimacy, and hence potential power, that is at present denied to a non-elected queen.

Thus, while it is possible to imagine a British republic, there is little reason to expect that any major party will press for one for some time to come. However, this does not mean that the monarchy will be able to stand still. An institution that some critics describe as a 'living fossil' must adapt if it is not to become a purposeless relic of past glories. It has not, of course, been stationary in recent years. Arguably, indeed, the institution changed much more in the second half of the twentieth century than in the first, and today it is staffed by people who take the need for further reform as seriously as anybody. The problem is not the monarchy's willingness to change – the difficulty is working out the direction in which the necessary change should go, and establishing the appropriate future role. If there are 'lessons to be learnt', as the Queen declared in her historic 1997 broadcast following the death of Diana, Princess of Wales, it remains unclear exactly what those lessons might be.

## Monarchy in the twenty-first century

In key ways, contemporary demands of the monarchy are mundane: people look not for mystery or magic, but for value for money. Stripped of almost all its former political functions, required to pay tax and make economies, the twenty-first century monarchy is required not only to be financially efficient and (up to a point) accountable, but also to be available to an ever wider public. Pressure for a slimmed down, more streamlined royal family will certainly increase, with demands for greater public access to palaces, art works and gardens. One possibility is a purely ceremonial institution, involving a titular headship from which all remaining discretionary authority is removed. Another, proposed by the late Lord Houghton in the early 1970s, would entail turning the Royal Household into a government department, with a 'Minister for the Crown' answerable to Parliament on matters affecting the activities and running of, and provision for, royalty.

Yet it is not inevitable that the institution must be hollowed out if it is not to disappear altogether. Defenders can point to the surviving scope for the sovereign, under certain conditions, to play a minor but significant role in filling the gap left by the modern electoral political system, which responds to the wants of mainstream voters, but can be insensitive to other needs. The acknowledged role of encouraging, warning and being consulted provides the monarch with a legitimate authority that can from time to time be used as a counterweight to governmental excesses, especially when the official Opposition is weak. Thus – without any public statement – the Queen was believed to be exercising such a role in 1986, when the subtlest of royal hints gave reassurance to Commonwealth members that Margaret Thatcher's hostility to sanctions against South Africa over apartheid was not universally shared within the British Establishment. In a different way, the Prince of Wales's 'Prince's Trust' has been remarkably effective in reaching deprived and alienated young people often ignored by a political system that (as the American economist JK Galbraith has pointed out, in a US context) favours the 'contented majority' of citizens who are more likely to take part in the political process.

History shows, however, that nothing can be predicted with certainty. It is a truism that an institution often derided for its conservatism has flourished because, in the end, it has always been flexible. The crisis of the contemporary monarchy has arisen, in part, because its historical twentieth-century roles have been superseded – there is no longer a need for an imperial leader or a 'head of society'; calls for patriotic leadership are fewer; and (for the time being, at least) the always somewhat unreal 'model family' concept has fallen apart. In 2002, the monarchy retains a high degree of public affection and support. But its long-term survival must depend on its ability to evolve, with greater alacrity than in the past, to the demands of a rapidly changing nation. Elizabeth II's Golden Jubilee finds the British monarchy in remission, after a bad patch. Can a postmodern version emerge, taking account of an ethnically diverse, anti-hierarchical society? The answer depends on a public mood that is hard to call, and on the behaviour, judgement and determination of those who guide, and embody, Britain's oldest institution.

*Ben Pimlott is Warden of Goldsmiths College and author of* The Queen *(HarperCollins).*

# Part 2

Confound their politics

# Heads of state

The president in a constitutional monarchy

**Graham Allen**

Those who are serious about democratic change in the UK do not have energy to waste attacking the soft target of the monarchy. In fact, it would be positively harmful to abolish the monarchy before codifying and limiting the mightiest office in the British state – that of the prime minister. Our biggest and most urgent challenge is to limit the UK's unrestrained executive.

Behind the comforting myths of parliamentary sovereignty, cabinet government and party democracy, we have allowed the office of the prime minister to become an executive presidency with a range of powers far beyond those of any other democratic political leader – including the President of the United States. This process has been going on for years, under prime ministers of all political parties. It did not start with Tony Blair. Similarly, when we examine the monarchy, we must examine the evolution of the modern British state.

Against that background, the monarch, as holder of the office of sovereign, does an essential if largely unacknowledged job in limiting the power of the prime minister, as holder of the office of head of government. She denies the prime minister the legitimacy and moral authority of being the head of state. Her existence ensures that the vital organs of the British state – the armed forces, police, judiciary and civil service – owe their appointment and loyalty to the nation as a whole, through its permanent head of state, and not to its temporary head of government.

Transferring this moral authority to current prime ministers would simply make our system of government even more unbalanced, unchecked and unseparated. It would also remove a flimsy but ultimate safeguard against the abuse of prime-ministerial power.

A lesser error would be to transfer the queen's power as head of state to a figurehead president. The process of replacing the monarchy would be immensely time-consuming and divisive and a distraction from the real agenda of democratic reform. When the process was over, all that we would have achieved would be to have given ourselves a replacement head of state with the same functions as the queen but with far less legitimacy, and no roots in our history.

It is far more important to look at the relationship between the monarchy and the prime minister. In particular we should examine the surviving prerogative powers of the Crown, which are laid out before prime ministers like a self-service buffet. They can help themselves to the prerogative virtually at will, to achieve acts of government for which they cannot be held to account.

### A unique job description

No other politician in the Western world does as many jobs as the British prime minister. He or she has a collection of offices that would make history's most absolute monarch salivate with envy. He or she is:

- Head of government, taking responsibility for every policy decision by the UK government.
- Chief ideologue of the British state, defining its values and purpose. The prime minister is expected to define and declare the priorities of government, its reasons for existence, the interests it aims to serve.
- Chief legislator in the government, determining its programme for each session and the content, timing and place of introduction of major bills.

- The UK's principal representative overseas on all issues of policy. In time of war or emergency, the PM is the country's *de facto* supreme commander.
- Leader, standard-bearer and principal advocate and strategist of his or her political party in the legislature and in the United Kingdom at large. For both government and party, he or she takes responsibility for satisfying the now almost limitless demands of the media.
- Finally, he or she is a constituency MP.

With this unique combination of functions comes a unique and awesome combination of virtual monopoly powers. In the seventeenth century, when a monarch ran the executive, the abuse of such powers resulted in the English Revolution. Now those powers – and some – have passed to the prime minister.

As a result, the prime minister has a unique power to appoint people as ministers, including those who are unelected through the House of Lords. The prime minister can reshuffle and dismiss ministers at will: the only constraint is the risk of unpopularity or disaffection.

The prime minister has undisputed control over the formal machinery of government, and the power to remodel or bypass it as a source of policy or advice. He or she controls senior appointments in the home civil service, the diplomatic service, the armed forces and (as far as Britain's quota is concerned) the European Union and other international organisations.

Although the present government has devolved power to Scotland, Wales and Northern Ireland, the prime minister can still choose to control and corral local government in England and to micro-manage the output of public services and state-run concerns.

Except for those originating in the European Union, the prime minister determines which laws are passed by the United Kingdom Parliament, and has the power of making and executing law and policy outside Parliament through the surviving prerogative powers of the Crown.

On the European and international scene, the prime minister ultimately decides what deals are struck, what agreements are signed, what commitments are made and honoured, and when the country's forces are used in conflict.

As party leader, the prime minister can now expect to determine the party's policy and ideology and choose its senior officials. If the party resists, the prime minister can make political capital by overriding the resistance. He or she can choose the party's political strategy and has privileged, if not unique, access to opinion research.

He or she can veto the party's parliamentary, European and even local government candidates and impose candidates on unwilling local parties. Once members are elected to the House of Commons, the prime minister, through the whips, has a vast array of patronage and threat to keep them in line. Incredibly, it includes the power to appoint them or refuse them as members of select committees. Prime ministers can choose which MPs have the most power to investigate them and their ministers. With the possible exception of North Korea, no other legislature in the world accepts such a humiliation from its head of government.

Finally – and most importantly – the prime minister has a supreme power to make and manufacture news. He or she can choose when to communicate personally and directly to the British people through the media, and how and when to put over a message or a story.

### The need for reform

Such a mighty office might once have been described as a monarchy; the most apt model today might be a presidency. It did not result from conscious annexation by individual prime ministers. It is not the result of the 'presidential' style of any individual. It grew from the needs of governing the modern British state – particularly during two world wars when all its resources had to be mobilised; of satisfying people's demand for higher living standards and better public services; and of servicing a mass democracy.

The biggest and most urgent task in our constitution is not to take cheap shots at the residual old executive – the monarchy – but to codify the powers of the modern executive, the prime minister, and decide how we want to make that office accountable. This rebalancing of our constitution is necessary to create an effective, trusted, admired parliament, and local and devolved governments and assemblies.

As a first step in that task, I introduced, in November 2001, the Prime Minister (Office, Role and Functions) Bill – the first attempt in modern times to define and legalise the prime ministership. The process led me to examine the surviving prerogative powers of the Crown, and how they are available to the prime minister.

It was a fascinating process. I found that no one has actually listed them. Eventually I came up with a group of 13. They range from the really important (making Orders in Council – that is making laws outside Parliament, declaring war, declaring a state of emergency, commanding the armed forces, signing treaties, recognising governments, appointing major public officials) to the weird and the wonderful, including the ownership of swans, whales and sturgeons.

This huge battery of power is presently outside the scope of parliamentary scrutiny. My bill aims to make the prime minister responsible for the use of these powers on his or her advice, rather than hiding behind the monarch's cloak.

Prerogative powers are the major means by which the monarchy bolsters prime ministerial power. In other important respects, the monarch acts as an informal check on prime ministerial power, and no one else can do it better.

First, the monarch advises and warns the prime minister and holds him or her to account at audiences. Many modern prime ministers have found this a more demanding scrutiny than that of Parliament.

Second, the monarch and the monarch's family share media attention with the prime minister. Without them, the prime minister would have an even greater dominance over the media.

Third, the monarch is an unacknowledged ideologue for the British state. Although the Queen never gives a political ideology to the British people, she regularly expresses fundamental values for the British state. Her presence embodies the values of duty and public service, and in countless speeches and public appearances she expresses core principles, including the rule of law, ethical conduct in personal and public life, and an inclusive view of British society. One does not need to defend the monarchy in its own right to recognise that its reform represents a distraction from the real test: caging the biggest beast in the constitutional jungle by addressing the unchecked and unregulated executive powers of the prime minister.

*Graham Allen is Labour MP for Nottingham North and served as a whip during the first term of the Blair government. He is author of* Reinventing Democracy *(1995) and* The Last Prime Minister: being honest about the UK presidency *(2002).*

# Monarchy and unionism

Eight different lives united under the Crown

**Ruth Dudley Edwards**

What do the following Northern Ireland unionists have in common?

*Charles* is a prosperous dentist in County Down who occasionally goes to a Church of Ireland service. He went to public school and Trinity College, Dublin, married a southern Roman Catholic and hugely enjoys rugby weekends in Dublin with Irish friends. Mildly left-of-centre, he is interested in British politics, wishes New Labour would stand in Northern Ireland and rarely votes as he finds Northern Ireland politicians appallingly provincial. Last year, however, he turned out for Lady Hermon of the Trimble wing of the Ulster Unionist Party (UUP), because he regards her as civilised and sophisticated. He thinks Ian Paisley is a Neanderthal bigot and he wishes that Orangemen would lighten up, stop parading and get a life.

*Joan* is also Church of Ireland but is devout. Her husband, a member of the Royal Ulster Constabulary, was shot in the head in the early 1990s as he patrolled the main street of a nearby Armagh village; his RUC colleagues could not charge Séamus, whom they knew to be responsible, as the witnesses were intimidated. Joan was brought up in a stoical tradition; she and her two children have never talked to the press about their grief, which became even more intense when Séamus was seen on television complaining of police harassment and brutality and demanding the disbandment of the RUC. He smiled at her once in a supermarket queue and she was nearly sick; he, of course, did not know who she was.

Joan has fought hard to live up to her religion and forgive, so she voted for the Belfast Agreement even though it involved early release for terrorists. She was very supportive of her best friend, Maureen, a Catholic and also an RUC widow, when her husband's killer returned to the neighbourhood after serving only two years. Joan had to endure Séamus being elected to the Northern Ireland assembly and, when the British government yielded to republican pressure and changed the name of the RUC, she and Maureen felt their murdered husbands had been retrospectively dishonoured by the British state which they had served. Instinctively conservative, Joan used to be a member of the UUP, but she can no longer bear to vote. She has never visited the Republic, which she believes harbours terrorists.

*Gardiner* is a Presbyterian who runs a farm in County Fermanagh that has been in his family since an ancestor left Scotland for Ulster in the seventeenth century. He goes to church every Sunday, is secretary of his local Orange lodge, likes to parade with his brethren a few times a year and, although he deplores violence, will turn up at Drumcree to show solidarity because he believes in the right of free assembly.

Gardiner gets on well with his Catholic neighbours but hates republicans, having seen several friends and neighbours murdered for the crime of being Protestants. His maternal grandfather, a member of the Royal Irish Constabulary, was murdered in Cork by the IRA in 1923, the rest of his family were forced to flee to Northern Ireland, and he hates the hypocrisy in the south that has airbrushed out the mistreatment of the Protestant community. He gets very cross when accused of being part of the Protestant Ascendancy which oppressed Roman Catholics, since discrimination against Presbyterians in the seventeenth century drove one of his ancestors to emigrate to America and, at the end of the eighteenth, another – attracted by the ideals of the French Revolution – joined the United Irishmen, rebelled against the British government and was hanged.

Gardiner felt betrayed when Margaret Thatcher, whom he admired, signed the 1985 Anglo-Irish Agreement which gave the Irish government a say in Northern Ireland policy. Still, he wants to live in peace with his neighbours and even though he hated the idea of seeing murderers – loyalist or republican – set free, he voted for the Belfast Agreement when Tony Blair promised that terrorists would not be let into government unless they had given up violence for good. He now believes that Blair is a liar who cravenly appeases violent republicanism, but, though he regrets voting for the agreement, he will continue grudgingly to support Trimble because he doesn't think Paisley's Democratic Unionist Party (DUP) is offering any viable alternative.

*Harold* is a Baptist and a retired post office manager with a deep interest in local – particularly military – history; his grandfather and two great-uncles were killed in the First World War and an uncle was shot down over Germany in the Second. Every year he visits First World War battlefields and memorials in France. He dislikes sectarianism of any kind, but he voted for the reasonable young DUP candidate in the last election as a protest against the British government, which he believes has ignored the sacrifices of the loyal people of Ulster and wants to sell them out along with their counterparts in the Falklands and Gibraltar.

*Jack* is a Free Presbyterian who runs a small shop in a small Protestant town in County Antrim and is a faithful religious and political follower of Paisley. He is standing for the DUP at the next election and sometimes finds it intellectually taxing to be standing on an anti-Agreement platform that calls for the abolition of the assembly he desperately wants to be elected to. A preacher with a good line in anti-pope jokes, his politics are entirely tribal: he hates the English, whom he considers as godless as they are treacherous, almost as much as the Irish, who he thinks want to force him to bow the knee to Rome.

*Davey* lives in East Belfast and though the expected job in the shipyard did not materialise, he was lucky enough to become a carpenter employed in the civil service. He abandoned his Methodism along with tribal politics when he became an enthusiastic trade unionist and communist, mellowing to socialism after the collapse of the Berlin wall. He has Catholic friends, but the rise of the rampant nationalism that is polarising Northern Irish politics and that makes the Republic of Ireland anathema to him has turned him off politics completely.

*Bobby* never goes to church, lives in a small Protestant enclave in North Belfast and is a bigot and proud of it. He knows that all Taigs, whether they call themselves nationalists or republicans, want to railroad him into the Irish Republic, which he believes to be run by paedophile priests and brown-envelope politicians. Although he was brought up to be proud of being British, he believes now that his government and the people of the mainland want to abandon the loyalists of Northern Ireland. He used to vote for the DUP, but he thinks they're all words and no action; he worships Billy Wright, the loyalist murderer who agreed with republicans that the British government responded only to violence. Wright's murder in prison by republicans gave him martyr status and he is Bobby's inspiration.

Bobby became involved in the Holy Cross protest for many reasons, including these: for years republicans had stopped Orange parades by threatening violence; Sinn Fein was on a roll and its leaders were hailed as peacemakers despite heading a still-active IRA; Protestants had been steadily driven out of West and North Belfast; republican thugs were daily intimidating people from the Glenbryn estate and stoning or bombing accessible houses; and no one seemed to care about the appalling deprivation and hopelessness of the loyalist population.

*Tommy* knows he's a Prod but could not even spell 'bigot'; he is covered with nasty tattoos, sells drugs, is a foot-soldier in the Ulster Defence Association (UDA) and spends quite a lot of time painting kerbstones red-white-and-blue, putting UDA flags up on lampposts, engaging in consensual rioting activity with young republicans and trying in concert with them to set the police on fire. He doesn't know the name of the British prime minister but he does know David Trimble is a traitor.

## How those eight Unionist paths cross

The Charleses would never have dinner with any of these unionists. They are sorry when told about the Joans, have heard of but never met anyone like the Gardiners, would consider the Harolds complete bores, find the Jacks an embarrassing joke, regard the Daveys as good sort of people but *so* 1970s and dismiss a Bobby or a Tommy as *Untermensch*.

The Joans, the Gardiners and the Harolds think the Charleses are privileged, selfish people who offered no leadership to the unionist people during the Troubles, thus leaving a vacuum for the Jacks. The Daveys are beyond their comprehension and they pray that the Bobbys and the Tommys will find religion and repent. The Jacks think the Charleses are traitors, the Joans, the Gardiners and the Harolds are milksops, the Daveys are godless and the Bobbys and Tommys are misguided – but what do you expect when you let Taigs push good Protestant people around? The Bobbys don't think about the Charleses or the Gardiners or the Harolds or the Jacks or the Daveys, they no longer have sympathy for the Joans because they hate the police, they dream about Billy Wright and new ways of fighting for Ulster, while the Tommys sell their drugs, hope to get rich and wait for their hero Johnny Adair to get out of jail and lead them . . . somewhere.

All that Charles and Joan and Gardiner and Harold and Jack and Davey and Bobby and Tommy and the rest of the Northern Irish unionist community have in common is the Crown. They will all have been saddened by the death of the Queen Mother but heartened by the manner in which she was mourned. Indeed, the sight of tens of thousands of British people queuing up to pay their respects will have given them all an injection of national pride and a feeling that perhaps after all loyalty is not a dirty word.

Charles has no particular interest in individual members of the royal family, but 'God Save the Queen' is a necessary part of his history and identity. Joan, Harold and Jack have all met members of the royal family and believe they have a genuine concern for their loyal subjects in Ulster and care about murdered soldiers and police and innocent civilians.

Gardiner particularly prizes the continuity offered by

royalty and sees an unbroken line from the Queen back to William of Orange. His submission to the Crown is, however, conditional, being based on the Bill of Rights of 1688, which requires the monarch not just to accept the supremacy of Parliament but to uphold the Protestant religion: Roman Catholicism to Gardiner is as redolent of autocracy, illiberalism and superstitition as it was when a distant ancestor fought against King James II. Davey thinks the monarchy is theoretically an anachronism but in practice a vital lifeline for unionists. Bobby and Tommy know that republicans are trying to take the Queen away from them and so are prepared to do anything to keep her.

Northern Ireland Protestants are fissiparous in the extreme. 'The unionist family', wrote a dispassionate insider to me recently, 'is a disparate confederation of political opinion ranging from left-wing socialism to right-wing extremism of National Front proportions. The sole unifying element within this broad spectrum is the Crown. Remove the Crown and unionism will fragment. Remove the Crown and the emblems of the Crown and unionists would be a people stripped of their constitutional clothes and would become politically naked.'

That, of course, is why virulent republicans have set out to strip the symbols of the monarchy from the police and the courtrooms and all public buildings: the objective is to hollow out unionists' sense of identity. Yet since unionists would as soon join up with the Netherlands as with the Republic of Ireland, there is no prospect of their swapping their Britishness for Irishness any more than the Falklanders will become Argentinians or the Gilbraltarians will say yes to being Spanish.

Take away the monarchy and you remove from one million people – around 20 per cent of the population of the island of Ireland – all sense of security and identity? What happens then?

*Ruth Dudley Edwards is an historian and journalist. She is author of* The Faithful Tribe: an intimate portrait of the loyal institutions *(HarperCollins, 2000).*

# Force of conservatism

The monarchy as politically powerful anachronism

**Stephen Haseler**

Anyone – and there were many – who truly believed that the British monarchy was an essentially unimportant institution, nothing more than a harmless hangover from olden times, needs – to put it politely – to seriously reassess that opinion. For the events of the spring of 2002 – the death of the Queen Mother and the preparations for the golden jubilee celebrations – make a powerful point: that Britain's lavish and archaic monarchy and royalty still not only suffuse, but dominate, our national life. The acres upon acres of press space, the over-the-top television scheduling, and the obsequious reporting by strangely termed 'court correspondents' tell us all we need to know about the continuing power and reach of this institution and family.

And the extraordinary spectacle of the recall of the British Parliament – our so-called 'forum of the nation' – not to discuss a looming world crisis but, rather, to pay individual tribute after tribute, only proves the point that monarchy may not be the trifle we are so often told it is, and can exert real influence over the political world.

That this huge national coverage – saturation coverage – of monarchy and royalty has no political consequences is still held to by monarchists. My colleague Professor Vernon Bogdanor is fond of pointing out that the Queen has no political influence because she makes speeches only, to use the technical term, 'on advice' – that is speeches written by ministers. Quite so. But this approach amounts to an extremely narrow reading of what constitutes influence in politics.

For instance, the life of our politics – its agenda, its context, its public opinion – is created in part by national mood and style set through the leading institutions and the mass media. And to believe that our lavish, highly intrusive (intrusive, that is, into our own lives) monarchy and royal family do not affect such mood and style is highly fanciful. It is equally fanciful to believe that such influence is not highly political. For instance, because of the royal family's continuing decision to overassociate themselves with national, indeed imperial, tradition – with all its ceremonial symbolism, images and flummery – they are, probably unconsciously, in serious danger of becoming a rallying point for nationalism, indeed xenophobia. And all this at the very time when Tony Blair is seeking to create a national mood in favour of joining the euro and integrating further into the European Union.

Monarchy in Britain which is not just feeding nationalism, but promoting what Tom Nairn has called 'the glamour backwardness' (rural nostalgia in an urban nation, heredity in a meritocratic age), thus becomes a real 'force of conservatism', perhaps more powerful than any other, certainly more so than the Eurosceptic Conservative Party. And with the Queen's head on the pound note, and the Queen still, extraordinarily among modern Western nations, commander-in-chief of the armed forces, the No campaign in the coming referendum must surely be thinking seriously about enlisting her.

In one sense the Windsors cannot help but enlist themselves on the side of the 'forces of conservatism and backwardness'. No matter who inhabits the throne, or who advises the monarch, the very institution of monarchy itself (as head of a unitary, centralised state, as head of the Commonwealth, as head of an established church, as the font of all honour and apex of our unwritten constitution) puts the monarchy – even before the Queen has said a word or Prince Charles given us a lecture – on a collision course with modernity, and particularly with any attempt to create a modern constitution for the British people.

As right-wing commentator – of the reactionary, not neoliberal kind – Bruce Anderson could write in the *Independent* on the day before the Queen Mother's funeral, and this is truly worth quoting and savouring, 'But the spirit of the British constitution cannot be found in the law books. It was expressed on Friday [in one of the ceremonials linked to the Queen Mother's death] by the young Princes, marching behind the gun carriage which carried their great-grandmother's coffin.'

## A dysfunctional family

There one has it: the unwritten constitution which governs us has nothing at all to do with parliamentary sovereignty, freedoms and human rights, the power of the people through the franchise; no, in this 'vision' the British constitution is all about one hereditary family. And in the process, of course, we also skew our view of our own history: what becomes important is not that aspect of British history which was about struggles for democratic reform – for parliamentary ascendancy over the Crown, or the end of the divine right of kings, or the extension of the franchise and women's rights – but rather the life of one privileged and dysfunctional family that happens to embody a way of life which conservatives feel is under threat.

When all is said and done, it is the British monarchy which ultimately blocks us from having a written constitution, a dis-established church and a sensible Commonwealth structure (in which the heads of state of other Commonwealth countries, including India and South Africa, would no longer be blocked by the British monarchy from assuming the headship themselves). It may be a bitter pill for the valiant reformers of Charter 88 to swallow, but no real constitutional reform, as opposed to clever tinkering, can be achieved without confronting the issue of monarchy – that is, seriously reforming it or abolishing it.

Yet few politicians, including dozens of good constitutional reformers, want to touch this subject. So there remains – in yet another testimony to royal power – the utterly bizarre spectacle of moderniser par excellence, Tony Blair, fresh from kicking the hereditary peers out of the House of Lords, declaring himself to be an 'ardent' monarchist. And of radical Liberal-Democrats who call for a modern constitution but send their supporters in all their finery to the fossilised Lords – the one and only 'house of nobles' still left in the whole wide world – yes, the whole wide world!

But perhaps the area where the monarchy most effectively exerts real political influence is, secretly, in its informal, behind the scenes activity throughout the political structures, but specifically in Downing Street, and on the sitting prime minister. Access is the key to political power in any modern political system. In Washington, to be located near the President in the West Wing is a battle that rages constantly among key political advisers – because access, 'face time', means influence. And the Queen and Prince Charles should not be underestimated here. The fact is that Britain's Prime Minister still has a weekly audience with the Queen and no communiqués are issued – so no one knows what is talked about. And anything can be talked about.

The Queen considers that her role to 'advise and warn' a prime minister is a real one: and no doubt she exercises it. Lowly elected politicians spend hours formulating policies, putting them into manifestos, whereas simply a royal nod or wink, or a carefully chosen word of 'warning' from a monarch to a prime minister can be just as influential. One can only speculate about what kind of 'advice' Prince Charles, should he become head of state, would give the prime minister on issues such as fox-hunting, the organisation of the Commonwealth, rural issues like foot and mouth disease – let alone personal tax questions. Courtier's courtier John Major had a 'private chat' – the euphemism for secret meeting – with the Queen to discuss royal tax status, and I wonder what will be said to Tony Blair when the tricky question comes up about whether the Queen should pay inheritance tax on her mother's estate.

The issue here is not some egalitarian outrage; rather it is simple belief in the rule of law, and the applicability of that law to every person in the land no matter what their wealth or standing. The struggle for the rule of law through parliamentary supremacy is, as Bruce Anderson might well agree, as British (and English) as you can get. It is one of the country's greatest of all historical achievements. Yet, such is the power of modern monarchy, no British prime minister has yet felt able to insist on putting it into practice when it comes to royal taxes or legislation which affects Buckingham Palace.

This relationship between queen and prime minister is at the very heart of our antiquated constitution and is, in today's world with its rightful concerns about accountability and secretive influence, highly odd. The press regularly gets upset about unelected businessmen getting access and influence in Downing Street – and in return getting special favours – but not unelected monarchs. All in all, I would suggest that on top of the important political influence of tone, mood and context, many sensitive specific political questions – from Commonwealth issues to constitutional questions (such as House of Lords reform, reform of the Church of England, and issues surrounding the Scottish Parliament) – the Queen is far more politically influential than half the cabinet put together! Nor should we forget that the Queen's one and only political speech took place during an earlier bout of Scottish independence when, in a none too disguised warning against Scottish independence, she intervened directly in the party political debate in Scotland to remind everyone that she was 'Queen of the United Kingdom of Great Britain and Northern Ireland'.

## Blair: the Queen was unamused

Perhaps though, the very best example of political influence is the fact that the monarchy has stayed untouched and unmodernised, except at the very margins. Incoming Prime Minister Blair in 1997, like any constitutional moderniser, would obviously have cast his eye on the monarchy. And following the death of Princess Diana, serious reform, if not abolition, was possible. But Blair drew back from such a course – although had the Queen herself agreed to help usher in a new constitutional era, it would have happened. But she has obviously not been amused, and will not be leading such a cause. Intriguingly, the royals set up the 'way ahead group' to discuss – among themselves – the future role of the monarchy, and in the autumn there is to be a speech from someone called the Lord Chamberlain who is going to set out some possible future marginal changes – one of which would allow Camilla Parker Bowles to marry King Charles – but this future vision will include nothing fundamental, such as abolishing the prerogative powers or disestablishing the Church of England.

Of course, those 'forces of conservatism' that wish to keep the country from modernising its constitution or from joining the euro (or from smaller things like banning fox-hunting) will, naturally, want to defend the British monarchy – and not just to keep it in being, but to promote it as a political force through its role as a moulder of political and cultural opinion.

To use the monarchy as part of an armoury in the British political battle may be acceptable during normal times. But times are not normal, for in the next few years the country faces historic issues that will determine nothing less than its future fate – and that centre on the whole question of the role of the British state in Europe and the world and the Scottish and Irish issues. These questions raise highly charged issues of sovereignty, patriotism, nationalism and national identity as never ever before. As a symbol of its particular brand of Englishness, as a focus for dwelling on past glories, indeed living in the past, the monarchy knows no peer. So, in this coming highly charged environment – in which English national identity itself is at stake – how can it possibly be said that the role of the monarchy, no matter what the intentions of its practitioners, can be neutral?

Some modernisers might argue – they do it with me all the time – that raising the issue of monarchy is not worth the candle, that, ultimately, it is counterproductive because it puts moderate opinion off the 'real' agenda for change and modernisation. But the assumption here is that the monarchy is indeed neutral, or relatively so, indeed trivial, indeed a mere decorative aspect of our political life! Maybe it used to be, but not today. For in the first decade of the twenty-first century – with our relations with Europe, and the constitutional futures of England, Scotland and Ireland all in the balance – the monarchy, this great 'force of conservatism', is very much a part of the game, a hugely influential player – even though it is unelected.

*Stephen Haseler is Professor of Government at London Guildhall University, and Chairman of Republic, the Republican Society. He is author of* The End of the House of Windsor *and other books on British and European politics.*

# Spinning the crown

A response to republicanism in the media age

**Michael Shea**

Perception is reality in the goldfish bowl of public life. *Time* magazine once wrote that 'greatness in the Presidential Chair is largely an illusion of the People'. Similarly, the French statesman Talleyrand once declared that 'Nations would be terrified if they knew by what small men they were governed.'

The making of leaders, hereditary or elected, is in the image that the public have of them. That image is nowadays focused through the camera lens or otherwise interpreted by the mass media. Behind the image, however, we have in Britain today a constitutional monarchy which works very well indeed. It is also a popular system. Despite the direst of warnings in the most republican of our broadsheets that the death of a 101-year-old lady would leave the nation cold, and that apathy would be the overwhelming public mood, the massive out-pourings and demonstrations following the death of Queen Elizabeth The Queen Mother demonstrated conclusively how wrong they were. We are, at heart, still a monarchical nation.

Subsequently, the same journalists tried to suggest that the tens of thousands who lined the banks of the Thames to file past the coffin were in some way not 'typical'. But what then of all those hard-nosed supermarkets and chain stores that closed that morning, because of the 'overwhelming demand from customers and staff'? Were they, too, untypical?

Of course, there was some hysteria and media hype. Yet while it is of course important to keep the role of a monarchical system under review, there is little public appetite to have to justify continually the role of the Crown in modern society. These are sad days for the republican cause. Outside the letter pages of the *Guardian*, it seems to have few adherents, particularly at times of national danger or high emotion.

## Procession of presidents

Debate about the value of any monarchical system has largely, in my experience, focused on the alternative. What do we put in its place? I have won several small arguments over the years by playing the simple, but highly contentious parlour game of asking whom others might nominate as their candidate for a British president. I invite readers to play the game too: President Thatcher, Kinnock, Major, Blair, or perhaps some superannuated bishop or High Court judge?

And then comes the question of fair and democratic process. Holding our freeborn democratic principles high, we gaze across the Atlantic and what do we see? We may recall the fiasco of the last US presidential election when that great nation hung its head in embarrassment at the voting system, highlighted by those strange pregnant chads of Florida. 'Thank God only one of them can win' read a Washington bumper sticker. And then we must also force into the equation whether George Bush Junior would be President if his father had not walked that path before him. The world is full of dynasties, not just monarchical ones, and familiar names of familiar families tread the same boards in the arts, in the City, in business, and, above all, in politics.

A third issue, vented in occasional waves of politically correct outrage, concerns the cost of the monarchy. In my day at Buckingham Palace, the civil list costs were about the same as the annual grant to the Imperial War Museum. And think of the burden to the taxpayer of funding a presidential election every five years or so. Having finally chosen a new democratic leader of the country, he or she (how about Mo Mowlam?) would of course begin the business of being president, which, with a prime minister in Downing Street, would consist of undertaking the duties of . . . um . . . a constitutional monarch.

I once had the splendid opportunity of watching, at close hand, that wonderful communicator Ronald Reagan being programmed for his work as President. His speechwriter, Peggy Noonan, has said, 'the battle for the mind of Ronald Reagan was like trench warfare in World War I: never did so many battle so hard over such barren terrain.' I heard briefing statements from his staffers such as 'Mr President, your thinking on the Middle East this morning is as follows . . .' or 'Here is this morning's speech, Mr President. Sorry you haven't had a chance to look at it before you deliver it,' and a hundred other examples of a democratic presidency at work.

I am no apologist for the scandals that have beset some of the younger members of the royal family over recent years. Much has been done that dangerously weakened support for the present system. But this is nothing in comparison with the scandals concerning their leaders that have rocked many republican nations in recent decades. The United States had Clinton, but look too at our nearest neighbours in France, Germany and Italy, where everything from financial skulduggery to sexual scandal has rocked those presidencies to their foundations. At least in the British system money was not usually at the root of the problem.

Every system has its faults, but the British one still has its periods of public acclamation and delight. The tens of thousands of people who crowded to see the Queen during her recent visits to Jamaica, New Zealand and Australia surprised the republicans in each country in turn, but they say something more. Yes of course, as the Queen herself has said, the future of the monarchy is up to the people there to decide. But Australia is not the only country to find that choosing the right leaders from among its own people sometimes turns out to be more contentious than the monarchy has ever been.

## Palace, press and people

We live, as I say, in a goldfish-bowl world where more reputations are broken on the *Today* programme and on television than in Parliament. Editors throne and dethrone at will.

Whether dealing with princes, footballers, politicians or pop stars, they create gods and then turn them into devils. The early editions of the Sunday tabloids on the night of Diana's death were more virulent than any I have seen, calling her every name imaginable for her dalliance with Dodi al Fayed, and for bringing the royal family into disrepute. From one edition to the next, she became the People's Princess. We are of course all more charitable in the shadow of death, as we saw again in the multiple pages of eulogies for Princess Margaret, about whom little good had been written in recent years. But then the newspapers are pastmasters at licking the rich and famous to death and beyond.

Consider the disadvantages of having a political figure as a head of state chosen by open election. We are hugely fortunate in our present system of having no conflict between the head of state and the prime minister, but that is something that happens fairly frequently in France and elsewhere. Of course, as heir to the throne, the Prince of Wales has been outspoken on a number of social and quasi-political issues where conflict with official policies has become apparent. But he is the first to recognise that, when and if he comes to the throne, he will, as we say in Scotland, have to 'haud his wheesht' even on matters about which he has strong personal views.

A final thought: because most of the popular agendas of the day are decided upon and heated up by the media rather than by government, the handling of the mass communicators becomes all important. If that does not exactly call for more royal spin doctoring, it does mean being more alert to the business of news management. By pulling the veil of mystique that surrounds the Crown back a little further from time to time, as is happening very effectively at the moment, the true benefits of the present system will continue to be properly recognised by the vast majority of the British people.

*Michael Shea is a former diplomat who was, for ten years, Press Secretary to the Queen. He is Chairman of the Royal Lyceum Theatre Company and is the Scottish Member of the Independent Television Commission.*

# Redefining merit

The monarchy as public servants

**Nick Bent**

The Duke of Edinburgh once remarked: 'it is a complete mis-
conception to imagine that the monarchy exists in the interests
of the monarch. It doesn't. It exists in the interests of the
people.' Just how much truth is there in this claim? To some
extent, it must be tested afresh in each generation. Currently,
one of the greatest challenges to the monarchy is a perception
that its primary beneficiaries are the royal family themselves.
With inequality still growing, and with evidence that social
mobility is slowing, what does it mean for the monarchy to
serve, and to be seen to serve, 'the interests of the people'?

Arguably, the potential exists for the royal family to
strengthen its popularity and relevance for a new generation
by taking its efforts to support charity and community work to
a new level. In recent years, the royal family has shored up its
position by becoming more emotionally engaged, especially at
times of crisis. Now the challenge is for them to become more
socially engaged. Building on the work of the Prince of Wales,
and other senior members of the royal family, the preservation
of the monarchy lies in leadership in public service.

This leadership is necessary because the context in which
the Queen and the royal family perform their duties is that of
a nation divided. Those at the top, with their ever more
luxurious lifestyles, are pulling away from the rest of their

fellow citizens. At the bottom, a significant minority – dispro-
portionately drawn from ethnic and religious minorities –
remain mired in poverty and social exclusion.

While the unique role of the monarchy is to represent every
section of society, there is a particular need for the royal family
to reach out, well beyond Middle England, to the most marginalised. In his book *The Culture of Contentment*, JK
Galbraith criticised the emergence of a 'democracy of the comfortable', where the majority are doing well. He suggests that
because the poor tend not to vote, their interests risk being
ignored by politicians.[1]

Although the current government has explicitly begun to
redistribute, far more radical measures are required to provide
conditions where opportunity is genuinely equalised. There is
no guarantee that at the next general election the comfortable
majority will endorse the steps taken by New Labour, let alone
the prospect of more. Given the fragility of a divided society, it
is in the interests of all the people that the underclass is not
utterly abandoned to electoral forces.

**The rise of the New Elite**
While advancement in British society still remains too
dependent on the wealth and education of parents, the factors
governing personal success have shifted dramatically since
1800. Compulsory primary and then secondary education, the
expansion of higher education, new technology, fierce international competition – all these variables have contributed to a
society where the process of advancement is technocratic and
transparent, and predominantly based on intellectual and occu-
pational ability. This new system has produced a remarkably
homogeneous New Elite who are the chief beneficiaries of the
current system of wealth creation, and who dominate commercial life and the professions. They are the top earners across a
wide range of jobs, from banking to journalism, medicine to
fashion, accountancy to retailing. Their material success is
largely a function of ability and effort: good brains outweigh
good breeding; and graft outweighs gentlemanliness.

The benefits created by this New Elite are manifold:
economic growth; a degree of social mobility; justice in the

1 JK Galbraith, *The
Culture of Contentment*
(London: Sinclair
Stevenson, 1992).

courts; medical advances; improved travel and communications; competent and honest civil servants; a disciplined and effective military; and so on. Meritocracy remains easily the most efficient way to organise society, although like democracy itself, the meritocratic system requires checks and balances. Social democrats are in the bizarre position of advocating greater meritocracy and equality of opportunity while simultaneously highlighting the limitations of this approach. What is being questioned here is not the basis of a successful individual's achievements *per se*, but the successful individual's attitude to those achievements and to those who lack them through no fault of their own.

British society has not provided any moral or cultural 'countervailing power' (to borrow another phrase from JK Galbraith) to an obligation-free sense of entitlement. We live in a country where the richer somebody is, the less they are likely to give to charity. This is in sharp contrast to the US, where a culture of philanthropy is strong among the old money of the East Coast and the new money of the West Coast. In the UK the Charities Aid Foundation has highlighted significant falls in giving from well-off, middle-aged baby-boomers – a demographic timebomb ticking away under the foundations of the voluntary sector.

The term 'the New Elite' was first used by the late Michael Young in his 1958 book *The Rise of the Meritocracy*. Young's book was intended as a warning that a narrowly construed meritocracy, framed in terms of IQ and productivity, provided no basis for social justice in a world where intellectual talent is unevenly distributed. He rightly predicted that in a meritocracy, those who fail to measure up would become relatively worse off.

The New Elite's self-confidence is rooted in the conviction that they have 'earned' what they have, precisely because it was not gained through inheritance or nepotism. In the absence of a compelling ethical narrative grounded in human dignity and equality, there is no reason to respect the losers, nor any inclination to pay taxes to support them or to give to charities that might help them. The fact that talent, like titles, is inherited is conveniently forgotten. The lottery of nature and nurture hardwires inequality into human society. A hospital cleaner may work even harder than a QC, but the rewards for the former are pitiful by comparison.

The cultural counterweight to this problem is a new, or rediscovered, definition of 'merit': one which breaks out of the confines of purely economic contribution and reward, and speaks more to the burdens of privilege than its benefits. We need a society where the greater one's opportunity to give – be it in time, money, energy or empathy – the greater the obligation to serve.

## A new spirit of *noblesse oblige*

At its heart, the success of the monarchy in the twenty-first century lies in this ultra-aristocratic bastion of the Old Elite educating the New Elite in *noblesse oblige*. By using their position of *inherited* privilege to champion an alternative attitude to *earned* privilege, the royal family could secure a new legitimacy in national life. The monarchy of the future should be about cajoling and inspiring, in word as well as deed, the New Elite to give more time and attention and money to those who are marginalised.

The Prince of Wales shows every sign of taking the royal vocation to service seriously, and this is the core lesson he will seek to pass on to his sons. Not content with supporting existing charities (he is patron of nearly 300), he has created several of his own. Most notable is the Prince's Trust which since 1976 has helped 500,000 disadvantaged young people get training, secure work experience or start a business.

In a selfish age, such a public-spirited vocation is profoundly countercultural. And only the monarchy is in a position to play this unique role as the ultimate pressure group in British society. Free from electoral and commercial pressures, it can take a long-term, interconnected view of the common good. The very permanence and independence of the monarchy gives a freedom to engage with every section of society. Nobody else can bridge the gap between the urban majority and the rural minority; no cabinet minister is in the job long enough to get to know every corner of the country; nobody other than the Prince of Wales could spearhead the multi-faith, intergenerational 'Respect' initiative. The notion of the monarch as figurehead has been mocked, yet in an age of welcome but dizzying diversity, a symbol of national unity and continuity becomes more valuable, not less.

Admittedly, living out this new definition of merit may require some lifestyle adjustments by the royal family. Writing shortly after the death of Diana, Jonathan Dimbleby posed some searching questions to the royal family:

> *Do its members come into close enough contact,*
> *often enough and in the right places, with the*
> *'ordinary people' of Britain? Could their contact*
> *be less formal, less obscured by dignitaries and*
> *officialdom? Do they bestow too much attention*
> *on the armed forces and not enough on the*
> *rough-and-tumble world of housing estates and*
> *inner-city schools? Do their holidays need to be*
> *quite so long? Do they need quite so great a*
> *revenue to furnish their material needs?*[2]

While the royal family should not become dull in pursuit of worthiness, conspicuous consumption must be minimised. A palace or two may have to be surrendered, and perhaps replaced with more modest royal residences in the Midlands and the North. Far greater use should be made of state schools and hospitals, and 'pomp and ceremony' should be restricted to state occasions. As much time as possible must be freed up for supporting the work of community regeneration across the country, and throughout the Commonwealth.

These are not new ideas, and the importance of the welfare and community function of the monarchy has been rightly emphasised by academics such as Frank Prochaska and Vernon Bogdanor. But this aspect of the visible life of the monarchy does require additional emphasis in an age of elitism. Amitai Etzioni, writing in the last Demos collection, called for 'a return to a sort of moderate counterculture, or a turn to voluntary simplicity'.[3] The challenge is not only cultural but also ecological. With natural resource depletion at a dangerous level, a sustainable future requires the 'dematerialisation' of the economy and society, with an emphasis on quality of life not quantity of

2 J Dimbleby, *The Prince of Wales* (London: Little, Brown, 1998).

3 A Etzioni, 'Sustaining the community of communities' in T Bentley and D Stedman Jones (eds), *The Moral Universe* (London: Demos, 2001).

things. We need to change our attitudes, learning to live more with less. Is it too much to ask the royal family to exemplify this, as an example to the never-satisfied New Elite?

### Charles III: a reign of public service?

Jonathan Dimbleby has written that the Prince of Wales has lived his adult life 'knowing that at any moment he might become Charles III, or that it may never happen at all. He has solved what would otherwise be a quandary by ignoring it much of the time.'[4] The Queen has neither any need nor any desire to abdicate, and the formal succession may be decades away. In the meantime, the Prince of Wales will increasingly hold his informal activist role in creative tension with his enhanced duties on the Queen's behalf.

Nevertheless, it is fascinating to speculate what the reign of Charles III might look like. As king he will have less freedom to innovate and to speak, but all Britain will know that his beliefs and passions remain unchanged. The British people are not accustomed to Charles Windsor staying silent, and a majority are glad that he vocalises many of their own concerns and hopes. The question is how, not whether, his beliefs and passions will be expressed.

King Charles III will certainly use his new role to place a higher value on public service in our national life. Other measures he might choose to take include:

- Scrapping the Order of the British Empire, a relic of an imperial era that means nothing to most people and remains offensive to some. In its place he could create the Order of Elizabeth or the Elizabeth Medal, a living memorial to the decades of dutiful work performed by his mother and grandmother.
- Granting royal charters to strategically significant organisations to boost their prestige. The National Council for Voluntary Organisations, Community Service Volunteers and Voluntary Service Overseas would be leading candidates for this permanent form of royal patronage.
- Extending Buckingham Palace's tradition of sending congratulatory messages to centenarians, by encouraging

4 J Dimbleby, see note 2

parents, guardians, teachers and youth leaders to nominate young people to receive a special Eighteenth Birthday Message from the monarch.

While these actions fall squarely within the prerogative of the monarch, there will be occasions when the king's views will be politically controversial. The Prince of Wales has been outspoken about issues such as the environment, organic agriculture, disadvantaged young people, architecture and biotechnology. Some measure of conflict with the governments he sees come and go is inevitable, and in some cases (as with his stance on genetically modified food) this will enhance the popularity of the monarchy.

Nobody doubts the irony, perhaps even the futility, of a wealthy and hereditary head of state seeking to check the material ambitions and selfish concerns of the most successful sections of society. In highlighting the needs of the marginalised, the monarchy may only heighten its own embarrassment of riches. In an age when deference is dead, popular discontent with the royal family may outweigh respect for anything they do. And the New Elite may ignore the monarchy altogether, because those who have worked hardest to be successful may increasingly resent the automatic privilege of the royal family.

Yet despite the risks of this public service model of monarchy, the only alternative is abdication or abolition. Given the scale of the challenge of achieving equality of opportunity, the monarchy has a vital role to play in building support for further political reform. Progressive politicians can introduce fundamental change, but they need allies to overcome the tyranny of the comfortable majority. A monarchy committed to being the subtle and sympathetic partner of social progress is surely a monarchy worth keeping and celebrating.

*Nick Bent is a Demos Associate, a director of Burson-Marsteller's Corporate Social Responsibility Unit and Chair of the Oxford-Kilburn Youth Club.*

# Part 3

May she defend our laws

# Family history

The role of the British monarchy in national life since 1750

## Jonathan Parry

In 1762, Oliver Goldsmith remarked that 'the Englishman is taught to love the king as his friend, but to acknowledge no other master than the laws which he himself has contributed to enact'. Since 1688 Britain has rejected royal absolutism and has been a constitutional regime dominated by Parliament. For at least 200 years after that, monarchs continued to exercise some influence, especially behind the scenes. But most power lay with cabinet ministers and elected MPs. 'Ministers are the kings in this country,' George II reflected in 1744.

It is a peculiarity of historical analysis of the British monarchy that its most fervent defenders and its most passionate critics share many of the same explanations for its survival, with the result that these explanations have become generally accepted in popular discussion. Both interpretations focus on the power of deference, of mystique and of antiquated, or invented, tradition. The argument of this essay is that the role, continuance and popularity of the monarchy in the last 250 years cannot be understood in those terms – not, at any rate, without insulting the intelligence of the British people. Rather, its success is because it has symbolised a representative, constitutional political culture. Monarchy has expressed that representativeness in three ways. It has stood for the identifying characteristics of the regime, including not least its liberalism; it has exemplified values which very many people have admired or shared; and its human character has allowed the man and woman in the street both to admire it and to be irreverent about it. These themes are discussed below.

But we also need to remember one fact that contemporary media hype is in constant danger of obscuring. For most of the time since 1750, monarchy has not been that important. Most people have not thought very much about it, and most of the political nation has known perfectly well that the king has little power. It would be misleading to assume that royalty occupied a larger place in people's thoughts at the time of Queen Victoria's death in 1901 than at the Queen Mother's in 2002. Equally, there is no reason to think that reverential interwar newsreel footage of monarch and family was much more representative of popular sentiment than is today's *Daily Mail*.

## Constitutional symbolism

Paradoxically, the first and historically most important role of monarchy has been to symbolise Britain's constitutionalism. In its relative powerlessness, it has embodied a crucial aspect of national identity.

In the eighteenth century, both Tories and Whigs, at different times, opposed the monarchy's interventions in politics. The Tories disliked much about the Hanoverian *arrivistes* who took the throne in 1714; from the 1760s, the Whigs interpreted George III's Toryism as an attempt to betray the settlement of 1688–9. For both groups, the monarchy's pretensions were 'un-English'. But this equating of excessive monarchical ambition with foreignness was only one side of the coin, and it was the other side that usually landed face up. For most of the eighteenth and nineteenth centuries, the predominant feeling was of enormous self-satisfaction at the British constitutional achievement. It was generally asserted that the British had found a stable way of checking abuses of power – by monarchs and others. The balanced constitution seemed to protect 'English' freedoms – of thought and of enterprise – while winning widespread popular respect for the rule of law. This, it was claimed, had allowed the English genius to flourish, and the nation to grow in global political and economic power. By the Victorian period, it was a commonplace that power lay with the people's representatives in Parliament, checking executive tyranny and protecting the freedoms of self-governing local communities. Britain was a 'crown'd republic', in Tennyson's phrase, guided by representative men both at Westminster and in town halls: Manchester and Birmingham were seen as the modern equivalents of those great Renaissance republics, Venice and Florence.

The constitutional monarch was the head and defining symbol of Britain's unique regime, and became the readiest point of identification with it. What really sealed this identification of monarch and British liberalism was foreign comparison, especially during and after the long war against the principles of the French Revolution and Napoleon's autocracy, between 1793 and 1815. Republicanism in France had led to anarchy, terror and dictatorship. By contrast, George III became the most immediately visible symbol of British stability, morality and freedom. In the nineteenth century, nothing contributed more to British constitutional self-satisfaction than the inability of the French to avoid a perpetual destabilising oscillation between autocracy and bloody republican uprisings. The Paris Commune of 1871 stimulated a republican movement among some British working-class people, but this merely doubled the force of the middle-class reaction in favour of the monarchy and even the scapegrace Prince of Wales. The Russian Revolution and the murder of Tsar and family had much the same effect in 1917–18. And it was the royal family's symbolic status as the homely antithesis of Hitlerian militarism, shrillness, savagery and decadence that did most for its image during the Second World War.

At times of crisis, the British state has been represented by a fallible, often unremarkable, largely powerless and speechless human being – one of ourselves. Such a person has been a fitting standard-bearer for a regime that has consistently rejected the heroic rhetoric of utopian dictatorships. The French were told to worship those noble but malleable abstractions, Liberty, Equality, Fraternity; the British gossiped about the mental health of Farmer George. Russia bowed down to

Communism and Germany goose-stepped into Nazism; George VI stammered for England.

But it is not just the monarch whose potentially overbearing ambitions have been checked by the British constitution. For all the current alarms about 'presidentialism', the constitution does remain 'balanced' in the sense that the monarchy has helped to limit the powers of the political class. For a start, the remit of that class in Britain would be much broader if elected figures rather than the monarch exercised her remaining constitutional powers – since, in the hands of active politicians, they would be potentially of immense significance. Moreover, the monarchy has validated institutions and values which are essentially independent of the state – in the process adding greatly to its own base of support. For example, it has encouraged the work of charities and other voluntary agencies, and publicised the idea of social service. By continuous and extensive patronage, it has strengthened many of the institutions of civil society – not just charitable organisations but vast numbers of other bodies from the Citizens' Advice Bureaux to freemasonry. In the process, it has won a large constituency of admirers, not least upper- and middle-class women, for whom voluntary institutions offered a social purpose long before most career paths were open to them. They have felt their labours validated by royal approval, not to mention royal garden parties and investitures. A second example is the monarchy's close involvement with the armed services, as figurehead and inspiration. Its military connections have contributed to the process by which the army and navy have remained at the same time unusually independent from those who actually exercise political power, and yet immensely loyal to a resolutely constitutional regime.

### Moral symbolism

The second main way in which monarchy has fulfilled a representative function is in the sense of upholding conventional bourgeois morals. Though the image of a religious, decent, hard-working royal family is sometimes presented as an invention of the 1930s and 1940s, it is in fact a much older notion, even if its plausibility has ebbed and flowed over time.

A virtuous domestic image was associated with George III – Farmer George – partly in an attempt to recreate the Tory patriotism of Queen Anne and partly in sympathy with the evangelical revival. But the publicity given to his son's debauchery and extravagance then weakened it. In the 1840s the middle-class press turned Victoria, Albert and their children into a model of thrift, domesticity and industry, thereby making a statement that after the 1832 Reform Act Britain had rejected the licentiousness of a selfish, immoral and unaccountable aristocracy. This image was successful, not least because Victoria and Albert shared most of those values. Hence the damage temporarily done to the Queen by the John Brown scandal after Albert's death, and especially by the Prince of Wales's gambling and sexual adventures. In 1870 he was attacked in radical journals as an irresponsible and idle aristocratic libertine like George IV, at the same time as he was praised in middle-class papers as a paragon of civic dutifulness like his father Albert.

In the 1910s and 1920s, George V's family in turn became a symbol of a reassuringly homely, dutiful and banal patriotism in a time of world war and socialist and Bolshevik menace. The King took an English surname in 1917; his children broke with precedent by usually marrying British people (and marrying them in public). George V attended the FA Cup Final and the Royal Command Performance; he rode around the British Empire Exhibition on a toy train. Many working-class as well as middle-class people responded to his fatherly presence with respectful affection. However his son Edward VIII found his respectable dullness outdated and uncongenial and, in consequence, many of the royal duties meaningless; he played dance music in front of the Archbishop of Canterbury. But his fashionable glamour seemed to the moralists in church, state and media to pose a dangerous threat. His removal was a coup on behalf of the old value system of unquestioning duty, religious observance and family morality.

This value system, immensely strengthened by wartime propaganda, has continued to shape Elizabeth II's reign profoundly – with diminishing benefits, though it would be extremely foolish to underestimate the respect in which she is held in Middle England. It is not those values, but the continuing and simultaneous association of the royal family with aristocratic culture and excess which has done a lot to keep republicanism alive. Yet what is striking about republican arguments is their antiquity. Over 200 years ago, Tom Paine made the same criticisms of the extravagance of palatial life, the unwillingness of the royals to pay their dues in taxes, the sponging habits of Germanic hangers-on in particular, and the narrowly upper-class leisure habits and irresponsible sexual mores of princes. Generations of royals have learned to marginalise such criticism by toning down their excesses and emphasising their dutifulness, respectability, domesticity and communitarianism.

### Mystique and the cult of personality

The third way in which the monarchy has remained relevant to ordinary lives is that as a system it is necessarily reliant on personality. Human beings are potentially fascinating – and inevitably flawed. The more reverential writers on monarchy often emphasise its mystique and lament the intrusiveness of modern media coverage of royal affairs which has stripped that away to reveal the mere person beneath. But this implies that the institution cannot survive without deferential reverence – which in any case was never as widespread as it appeared. And the power of mystique can easily be exaggerated. A lot of the popular admiration for the royal family has been based on a very secular liking for individual elegance and stylishness – together with the occasional fantasy dream of a luxurious lifestyle. It is true that the monarchy has always had a religious character, symbolising the divine presence in national life and the duty of self-sacrifice for the community. But in modern England, establishment religion has traded much more on civic duty – with which the Queen is still strongly associated – than on mysticism and majesty. Archbishop Fisher believed that he had turned the 1953 Coronation into a religious act of 'national communion', but if he had, it did not last. Indeed he was attacked two years later for his inhumanity in preventing Princess Margaret from marrying a divorcee. Similarly, after the Abdication of 1936, the public was less censorious of the Duke of Windsor than of his overtly moralistic enemy Archbishop Lang. And the Duke was disliked more for being a shirker than for his taste in women.

Fascination with royal doings has been inspired less by mystique than by a universal interest in human stories. Irreverence, in the form of gossip and prurience, has been as important as reverence in keeping the royal family news-worthy. Princely laziness, extravagance, arrogance and ill-treatment of women have frequently been pilloried with relish. In the 1820s, George IV was satirised more viciously than any present-day royal. The tendency to lampoon 'important personages' and their toadies has been an immutable characteristic of modern British political culture. It has been an important clause in the unwritten contract between monarchy and people since 1688 that the Crown is held, not just on sufferance, but as a legitimate object of popular rebuke, a symbol of a free political society. Conversely, the ingredients of royal popularity, at least in the last 50 years, have been qualities to which the mass of the public can relate. These include, most obviously, emotional warmth and the common touch. Beyond that, respect has been won by a devotion to social service which can be seen as doing a job like everyone else. And displaying the pain of vulnerability and suffering – as long as it is met courageously, without self-pity – can move the sympathetic (and satisfy the jealous).

People relate to royal personalities in a host of different ways. This has been made much easier by the increase in media coverage. Royalty is much more apparent to ordinary people than it was in 1960, just as in 1960 it was much more apparent than it had been in 1880. This intense exposure has not neces-sarily diminished respect for the monarchy. Rather, its signifi-cance is twofold. Firstly, it has unearthed and broadcast a range of opinions that has always existed and has given them all a rather ponderous significance. In the process, it has made decided expressions of support for the monarchy, and opposi-tion to it, seem more widespread, and perhaps more strongly held, than they probably are.

Secondly and more importantly, it has made royalty infi-nitely more accountable to the people. In fact, relentless media scrutiny has forced the monarchy to be one of the most democratic and adaptable institutions in modern Britain. It is quite unrealistic to expect it to represent the full gamut of public opinion in modern society. Only the fawning or cliché-ridden call it the incarnation of Britishness; indeed it has never sought to reflect the scope of a tolerant and diverse society. But through its historical associations, its range of voluntary connections, its concern with social service, its exemplary values and its imperfect but usually dutiful individuals, it has been more representative than any other single totem. It does not intrude very strongly in most people's lives, but to the extent that it does, it mostly projects the benign qualities of Oliver Goldsmith's friend. Though the private views of the royal family have mostly been Tory, its public face has been continuously Whig. It has arguably been the most successful Whig institution in British history.

*Jonathan Parry is Reader in History at Pembroke College, Cambridge.*

# A queen's ransom

The economics of monarchy

**Evan Davis**

How much is the royal family worth to the British people and the British economy? It's always tempting to ask whether an institution is profitable for the nation, and indeed, in arguments about the royals, defenders can often be heard articulating vague assertions about foreign tourist revenues and the like. So how seriously should we take the economic arguments for the monarchy?

My view is that the royal family probably provides value to the nation well in excess of its cost, although tourism would only form a small part of that. But before outlining this particular argument, it is important to understand why no precise or objective economic assessment of the royal family can be performed.

## The limits of cost-benefit analysis

Economists are rightly proud of their skill at assessing the value of major public assets; perhaps the most famous was the cost-benefit analysis of the Victoria line, a new route for the London Underground, which was decisive in getting it constructed back in the 1960s. Such analysis, which is complicated to apply, looks at the costs of the asset (be they cash costs or hidden costs) and at the gains expressed in monetary values. These gains might be to users of the asset, or to others who don't use it (car drivers, for example, enjoying less congested streets as a result of the Victoria Line). In many cases, cost-benefit studies ask people how much they would be willing to pay for the services of an asset in order to derive notional estimates of the revenue that would be generated by it, even if those revenues are not actually going to be collected.

However, just in case a few simple-minded republicans are confused about this, the monarchy is *not* an economic asset like the Victoria Line. To ask people, 'how much would you pay for the pleasure you get from the royal family' is to pose a rather difficult question, and rather misses the point of the royals, who would not be as regal if we had to put a price on them. The mere act of imagining the commercialisation of the institution is to belittle its value. Nonetheless, whatever the difficulties of extracting meaningful 'willingness-to-pay' numbers from people, to assess the economic value of the royal family without taking into account the undoubted pleasure that it gives to a substantial proportion of the population would be absurd. The sense of worth which many in the nation derive from royalty is probably where most of its value lies.

But we also have to ask about the people who dislike the institution. There are undoubtedly some who would happily pay something just to see the royals abolished. Should those negative feelings be quantified and subtracted from the feelings of pleasure that royal supporters get to arrive at some net figure of overall pleasure generated? Personally, I doubt it. Sure, if the royal family causes substantive inconvenience or displeasure – for example, if ceremonial occasions disrupt traffic – the inconvenience ought to be considered as a negative in the economic assessment of the institution. But simple dislike of the institution is harder to account for. Those who derive no pleasure from the royal family are quite entitled in our country to ignore it. It seems to me that the appropriate treatment of republican sympathies in an economic assessment is to say that people are entitled to place a zero value on the institution, but not a negative value. But I can see that republicans might suggest this would rather skew the result of any economic assessment.

Even if one was willing to override these arguments and attach an economic *benefit* to the monarchy, it is still hard to assess the *cost* of the royals. How does one apply a true monetary estimate of the 'cost' to the nation of bestowing Windsor Castle on the royals for example? Many of the assets over which the Queen has custody have a value that primarily derives from their royal connection. If there was no Queen occupying Windsor Castle, one suspects there would be less interest in it, and the 'value' of the asset to a republican nation would be correspondingly reduced. After all, Britain has plenty of castles already. What it doesn't have is many *royal* castles.

## The economic impact of the royal family

There is another important reason why a normal cost-benefit analysis would be controversial. When economists assess the value of the Victoria Line, they add up the costs and benefits, usually ignoring the issue of who pays those costs or gets those benefits. Typically, for example, they do not mind whether the Victoria Line helps shops, commuters, homeowners or car drivers. A benefit is a benefit that needs to be quantified, just as long there is somebody who enjoys it.

Alas, if one applied this rule to the royal family, one would not necessarily judge the cost of keeping the royal family as a cost at all. After all, the civil list is a cost to the taxpayer, but a benefit to the royal family: the average taxpayer loses a bit of income, the royal family gains a bit of income. In pure economic terms, the loss and the gain cancel each other out. Hence, the cost of the civil list would not necessarily affect an assessment of the overall *net* benefit or cost of the royals. This simply tells you that economists are not qualified to assess whether a straight handout from some people to other people provides a net benefit to society as a whole. It all depends on how much you like the people to whom the money is going. But whether you value the money that goes to the royals is essentially to ask whether you support the royal family, which takes you back to questions economists can't be expected to answer objectively.

If no uncontroversial economic assessment of the royals can be made, it is still worth outlining some basic facts and figures, to provide indicative estimates of whether they are of economic value.

Perhaps the first and most striking point to make is that the royal family is not particularly expensive. The *Sunday Times* Rich List, published in April 2002, ranks the Queen at 125th in the UK with a net worth of £275 million. (Other royals do not appear in the list.) More relevant than the Queen's net worth, however, is her income. An official statement of Head of State Expenditure financed by public funds was issued last June, estimating the cost of the royal family in 2000/01 at about £35 million.[1] One might take that as the basic 'cost of the monarchy'. Most of this derives from the civil list (capped at £7.9 million a year until 2011); and grant-in-aid for maintenance of the royal palaces (£15 million a year, but not used for the Queen's own residences of Balmoral and Sandringham) and support for royal travel (about £5 million).

However, this understates the royal family's income, which is substantially supplemented by private funds, that could be said to add about £25 million on top of the taxpayer support.[2] Contributions to this include the profits Prince Charles enjoys from the Duchy of Cornwall, which yields about £6 million (although note the Prince is not allowed to keep the proceeds of any sale of the Duchy and thus does not 'own' the estate in the normal sense of the word). The Queen has private investment income, probably amounting to about £5.5 million; she also has her own properties that give her an income-in-kind. The family also has use of the state palaces as residence and office space (a thousand people work at the occupied palaces), which one might say is worth several million pounds a year. And the Queen derives an income from the Duchy of Lancaster, which was about £7.3 million last year. In addition, the Queen has privileged access to the Royal Collection, even if, again, she could not be said to 'own' it.

All in all, between the taxpayer support for the royal family, and the private and quasi-private income, one gets to a total annual income for the family (including a notional rent for all the palaces of about £5 million) of about £60 million. This conveniently equates to an annual cost per citizen of about £1 each, or 2p a week.

Needless to say, at this level, cost should not be much of a factor in one's view of the monarchy. If one were in the

1 These figures are drawn from the section of the royal family's website devoted to the royal finances, www.royal.gov.uk/output/page308.asp. I am also grateful to Jules Margo at Demos for help in collating some figures.

2 This figure is a heroic estimate, but it is within the right scale to be consistent with the *Sunday Times* net worth figure of £275 million. A sum of £25 million a year amounts to a rate of return of 9 per cent on £275 million, which is high but at least within the right ball park.

business of performing 'willingness-to-pay' studies, only 10 per cent of the population would need to derive £10 of annual pleasure from the existence of the Crown for it to be worth keeping at its current size and status. I suspect, given the attention and affection the family attracts, that the pleasure the monarchy gives the country accounts for this cost several times over.

And this argument does not take into account the fact that abolishing the monarchy would not lead to savings close to either the £35 million or £60 million cost estimates. After all, many ceremonial functions would have to remain (assuming we still invited foreign dignitaries to dinner, for example). And we would still have to maintain the royal palaces (assuming, I hope, we would not pull them down in a fit of anti-royal pique). And the Windsor family would surely keep quite a few of the assets and income included in my assessment.

## Tourism and services

What about some of the other arguments concerning the economic impact of the royal family? Around 25 million foreign visitors arrive in the UK each year, generating £12.8 billion of spending.[3] About 9 million of those travellers are holidaymakers, and thus one might suppose tourist revenues to be about £4 or £5 billion a year. Crucially, however, the actual benefit is of an order of magnitude smaller than this sum, as the tourist industry would be earning other revenues were it not helping tourists. One might, heroically, call the 'surplus' of tourism, over and above any income that would be generated by other activities, about £500 million a year. In that case, for tourism to pay for the monarchy, you would need to assume that about 10 per cent of tourists are coming here because of the royals.

My sense is that most tourists do not come here for the monarchy, *per se*. But many more than 10 per cent of tourists come here on account of a general feeling that Britain is a glorious heritage centre, to which the monarchy makes an inestimable contribution. Of course, were we to become a republic, it is possible that the mere legacy of a monarchy might achieve most of that, so I am not someone who believes we should

3 Figures from the year 2000, published in *Overseas Travel and Tourism, Business Monitor* MQ6, Q3 2001, from National Statistics.

preserve the institution purely as a tourist attraction. But it does seem right to argue that tourism goes a small way to defray the direct economic cost of the monarchy to the UK population.

A third economic value of the institution derives from the direct services performed by the royal family. According to Sir Michael Peat, Keeper of the Privy Purse, there are about 3,000 royal engagements a year. No one would seriously advocate that the monarchy should be charged out, or services privatised. But my personal view is that the benefit to society of having a royal family to perform the engagements they do is easily worth the money we implicitly pay for those services in state support.

This is because every society needs some way of providing civic institutions with a means of infusing themselves with glamour. A charity ball, for example, with a big name attending is perceived as a much more serious event than one without. A hospital wing opened by a celebrity gets some kudos attached to it that would otherwise be missing. All in all, society needs ceremony, symbols and stars to sprinkle a little magic dust over its affairs. The royal family provides this in spades. Getting a royal to open a hospital ward or a gala charity event is worth a great deal in distinguishing that event from the everyday. The monarchy thus travels the country, decorating society, adding colour and dignity to everything it touches.

Of course, the private sector can provide this kind of glamour too. In the absence of royalty, there are top-flight celebrities who can add a bit of star quality to a function, or whose name on a letterhead as patron of a charity is very helpful. In the United States , Hollywood generates a lot of star quality that gets spread around the country. Some might conclude that the private sector does this so well that a system of state-financed ceremony and majesty is quite unnecessary. Robbie Williams, for example, will do the job without taxpayer support. But I am sceptical. Robbie Williams is a big name. But he is no royal. For one thing, a possible drawback of private sector glamour is that it can be purchased for a price. This gives the rich, the corporate and the well-endowed civic institutions an advantage in obtaining the glamour that I am talking about.

So the value of the royal family is firstly in providing that function in a much more majestical way than any 'celebrity for hire' possibly could. And secondly, in allowing the non-commercial sector the chance to obtain that service, precisely because the royals are not for sale. While I would guess that the royal family could earn their keep in charging for appearances, and for putting their name on letterheads, our society is (literally) immeasurably richer for having an institution that does not charge for that service and which offers it to civic institutions such as hospitals and charities which might otherwise not get it at all.

And just to provide guidance on the value, if we accept the annual cost of royalty as between £35 and £60 million, the cost per royal engagement lies between £12,000 and £20,000. I would argue that up and down the land there are institutions touched by the monarchy that derive at least that kind of value from it. To put it another way, for £12,000 one would not be able to hire a private celebrity of anything like royal stature on the open market.

## The scaled-down monarchy

Of course, even if the royal family costs relatively little compared to the scale of public affection for the institution, it could in principle be delivered at an even lower cost. A really detailed study of royal finances would need to find not simply that the cost is low, but that at the margin, the cost is worthwhile. In other words, if we cut the overall cost of royalty by £10 million, would the benefits of monarchy fall by less than £10 million? If so, the option of 'scaling down' the resources absorbed by the monarchy would make sense in pure economic terms.

But it is hard to assess whether that is the case. It is true that, in the last decade or so, the cost of taxpayer support for royal functions has more than halved, with little diminution of the institution. One does suspect, however, that a 'monarchy on the cheap' could carry far less kudos than a quite expensive one, and because I view a major function of royalty as spreading colour and majesty around the land, I am personally sceptical that a bicycling monarch would really do the trick. In any case, as one of the largest monarchical economies in the world (and that does not even take into consideration the Commonwealth), it is not outlandish to argue that we can expect to have one of the more expensive monarchies.

## Conclusions

So, to summarise, there are three main benefits from the royal family which make it good value for money. Tourist profits probably offset a small share of royal expenses. The mere pleasure that supporters of royalty get from the institution probably more than justifies the total expense. And thirdly, the function performed by royal engagements probably goes a long way in generating value equivalent to the cost of the family.

The assessment I have provided is, of course, entirely subjective. One might take a contrasting view of the magic the royals provide, the pleasure they give and the value of a tourist industry based on heritage. But then, you could never look to economics alone to provide a justification for the royal family.

Royalty has a difficult time in an age in which deference has diminished and the cult of celebrity has developed. But there are deficiencies in the private sector market for celebrities. And for a reasonably modest cost, we have something far grander, far less commercial and more genuinely publicly owned than anything the private sector could provide.

*Evan Davis is an economics journalist.*

# Natural born monarchs

Can biology help us understand the role of royals?

**Richard Webb**

What does the science of biology have to say about monarchy? The unconsidered answer may be 'not a lot'. After all, monarchy is not a biological construct. 'King of the Beasts' and 'Monarch of the Glen' are mere figures of speech. Queens, as in queen bees, are valid biological terms, but the entomologists who thought that the bees offered us a model for living are all long dead.

A more considered answer is 'rather more than you might think, or want to believe'. One might suggest that what biology has to offer will one day change the way we all look at society and institutions.

Not that the social scientists want to hear it. Any biologist expressing a professional view on human societies and institutions is soon reminded that he or she is breaking a taboo. This is the taboo against viewing people as if they were animals, and supposing that the human mind and human culture are in any way the products of a natural process of evolution. In a curious inversion of other taboos, biologists today are permitted to study people's intimate body parts, but not to engage with their evolved minds.

Such reactions have deterred many a psychologist and human scientist from applying the powerful and tested methodology of evolutionary biology to human behaviour and societies. Speculating on the connections between evolution and monarchies as institutions is therefore a risky business. So let us invoke an extraterrestrial scientist, willing to think aloud, yet far enough removed to be clear of the inevitable fallout. An inhabitant of our neighbouring galaxy Andromeda, say. Let us suppose she is a naturalist who has been studying our planet's species for a few million years. As a sound biologist, she has a good grip of evolutionary theory but very little interest in sociology.

To her, we are just one species among millions, interesting but not that unusual. She sees a mid-sized, social primate with an unexpectedly large cerebral cortex. We happen to have wiped out all our hominid relations, so we look more peculiar than would otherwise be the case. Our nearest surviving relations are some rather specialised forest-dwelling apes, themselves not far from extinction.

That outsized brain is odd. It delivers much less practical advantage than we might suppose. For the 90 per cent of the time that our ancestors have been indistinguishable from us today and for the 99.5 per cent of the time that the human species has been recognisably human, we have hunted little better than wolves, foraged little better than pigs, and thrived in few more environments than rats.

What price the intellect? In many ways our brain appears to be a costly disadvantage. It is fragile, expensive, dangerous to the mother at birth, and dreadfully distracting. So, as with the peacock's ludicrous tail (which actually reduces flying ability), we have to look beyond practical functionality for a rationale.

Our Andromedan naturalist is clear that our enlarged brain evolved principally because it gave selective advantage in social contexts. The social environment is the primary competitive arena for most animals, especially a species as social as ours. One human's major competitor is another human. This is so, even against external forces like famine or predation. Who has a claim to the last scrap of food? Who is allowed into the cave at night? The competitive (and cooperative) arena is social.

Big brains (and brilliant minds) gave our antecedents the ability to show off, to flirt, to flatter, to tell stories, to form alliances, to do deals, to cheat, to bully, to wage war, and to turn lost causes to advantage. And to get more sex. Or rather, bigger brains enhanced those abilities. Humans that were better at doing these things tended to survive better, and to leave more descendants. New genes that promoted such traits spread, and over time became the norm in the population. Those turbocharged show-offs became our ancestors. This is evolution by natural selection. It is a slow process, with little change apparent in a thousand generations. And yet it does move.

## Monarchy and cultural evolution

What then of culture, social structures and institutions? Naturally, for millions of years our Andromedan has also been observing human culture evolving. Many other species have cultures: consider the whales' songs, the sheep flock's collective memory of its terrain, or the tool-using tricks of the sea otters. Such rules and know-how are passed on by cultural transmission, not genes, but are always closely linked to the behavioural imperatives and capabilities of the species involved.

True, no other species has anything as complex as human culture. Though we, like many animals, depend on cultural continuity, many gaps and losses can be quickly patched up. Examples of this are the ways that abandoned groups of children develop their own languages, and isolated tribes reinvent social structures.

Evidently, many cultural components and social institutions recur time and again. Monarchy, in its various forms, is one of them. Anthropologists can study this only by looking across today's impoverished range of human cultures, or peering into recent history. But our postulated naturalist has been watching us for far longer. She is in no doubt that the common structures of human culture reflect the distinctive nature of the human mind. Over the long view of evolutionary time, cultures and genes, people and practices have been favoured and embellished by natural selection to give the roots of today's diversity.

So, the present human institution of monarchy surprises her not at all. It is consistent with well-understood aspects of human social behaviour. Though not the only way of arranging things, leadership roles like patriarchs and matriarchs, chiefs and headmen have been a common theme for as long as she has been studying humans. That class of institution we would today call monarchy, she sees as an unremarkable subset of a very familiar pattern.

Elements of this pattern are to be found right across the living world. The most dramatic examples (for a non-biologist at least) come from other complex social animals, such as chickens and chimpanzees, dolphins and wild dogs. But the evolutionary specialist finds certain elements that are almost universal in living things, including social insects and flowering plants.

Notions of status and hierarchy are commonplace in social creatures. The pursuit of wealth is normal, and riches may be signalled by displays of conspicuous consumption. Status brings power and sexual advantage; droit de seigneur is rampant. Though the notion of 'good breeding' is not quite how a biologist would express it, the pursuit of genetic quality is found in even the simplest animals and plants. Quality is signalled in many ways, including flagrant acts of artistry and altruism. Top status may be indicated by demeanour, by external paraphernalia such as crests, and by the public exercise of exclusive privileges.

### Lineage and leadership

Kin and lineage are concepts central to all of evolutionary biology. The offspring of high-status individuals may inherit social advantages, quite apart from their genes. Nepotism is rife and dynasties are not unknown. One mechanism for the inheritance of social advantage seems to be higher expectation of status (and a greater willingness to fight for it) among those brought up by one or more high-status parents.

The role of paramount leader, acknowledged by the wider group, is not uncommon. Leadership authority is often gained initially through violence, which may be ritualised. In the more political species, alliances are common, loyalty is rewarded and revenge long planned. Brothers often make the staunchest allies.

Once gained, leadership authority in many species is sustained through a form of consensus. The leader cannot rule by force alone, and if he (tyrants are usually male) tries to, he may face a revolt by the masses (often orchestrated by the upper middle rankers), leading to his overthrow, disgrace, and even death. The group consensus may be manipulated in Machiavellian ways by the leader and his (or her) supporters, and by aspirants biding their time until they are better placed to topple the incumbent.

Duties may be expected of leaders, in the absence of which their authority may be forfeit. These duties can include prominent aggression in times of war (in those rather few species that go in for such planned violence against conspecific groups). More generally, the leader is active in the settling of internal disputes, and in particular the meting out of rough justice against bullies and cheats, and the comforting of victims. In these and other ways, leaders are instrumental in setting the moral tone of the group. Although accorded many personal privileges, they are expected to be just and fair, and to implement the rules of morality (as recognised by members of the group).

Well-led groups tend to flourish, more for social reasons than because of the practical direction their leaders provide. Individuals suffer less stress, disputes are better contained, and there is a lower level of background violence (especially from pre-adult males) where leadership is effective. The older females in particular value this stability, and may act to thwart the ambitions of a usurper. Wisdom and age are positive attributes in a leader, and grey hairs command respect. Real grief may be felt at the untimely death of a leader.

### Biology lessons for social scientists

Those examples all come from non-human species. Social biology is rich in examples of what look like the primary drivers of those human behaviours that characterise the institution of monarchy. Contrary to the public myth, such phenomena are not train-spotters' lists of observations from the animal kingdom (*sic*). Scientific methodologies are well established to explore, test and predict the connections.

Modern evolutionary theory, though rooted in Darwin's original insights, has in recent decades borrowed heavily from game theory and economics in particular. Outsiders are often surprised to discover that evolution is much more about outcomes – why things are as we find them today – than about fossils and family trees.

Our Andromedan biologist might struggle to understand why these methodologies and insights should be so repugnant to the social and political scientists who study the institution of monarchy. What could be more relevant, radical, and fun to apply than game theory, trade-offs, reciprocal altruism, kin selection, mating systems, female choice, parental investment, sex allocation, honest signals, the handicap principle, utility functions, or evolutionary arms races? The social sciences don't know what they are missing.

The stated objections appear perverse and metaphysical. Something to do with the conundrum of free will? The separateness of the human mind from the human brain? Or the difference it makes to know that we are conscious? However, she would concede one justifiable area of difficulty. The cultural explosion of the past few millennia was very startling, and has quite spoiled some of her experiments. She still wonders why this step change in technology, farming and writing should have happened just when it did, and whether she could have foreseen it. Nothing like this has happened on Earth before.

The outcome for us is a world very different from the one our species evolved in. A world in which the link between status and reproductive success may not (for a few generations at least) strictly apply. Contraception in particular screws things up. Mass communication shrinks the world. Written records sustain practices that would otherwise be forgotten, and allow institutions to self-perpetuate. Science takes us to new places, where we reason in ways that no craft, mythology or intuition could ever have suggested. Medicine keeps us alive, and technology is running away with itself.

In such a world, many assume that evolution has little to tell us. And yet, people are still people. See how well our infants cope, born into a lifestyle so different from the Stone Age one for which we are all adapted. As we know, it is the social world that is the human's primary environment. For all its sophistication, today's culture still follows the old patterns.

Read a newspaper, contest a will, grab some fast food, or attempt a seduction, and you will find the old universals – rules and preoccupations and reactions – coming through loud and clear.

Human behaviour, society, culture and institutions are not independent of people, and can only be properly understood in the light of human nature. For reasons of historical and political accident, many of the best tools for analysing and exploring human nature are in the hands of biologists. Maybe biologists are not the best people to be commenting on the institution of monarchy. But until the social scientists adopt their methodologies for their own disciplines, they will find that biologists go on having too much to say about people.

© RH Webb 2002

*Dr Richard H Webb is a Visiting Research Fellow at the Centre for Philosophy of Natural and Social Sciences, London School of Economics and Political Science.*

# Parks and palaces

How monarchy reigns over public space

**Terry Farrell**

The monarchy continually has to adapt and change. This applies not only to the royal family as an institution, but also to the spaces it owns and inhabits. In recent months, I have put forward a number of proposals, most notably in the Channel 4 documentary *The Palace Redesigned*, aimed at opening up a debate about the use of these spaces. My argument is that revamping Buckingham Palace and its surroundings to make it more permeable to the people would be a symbolically open gesture for the monarchy. Urban design has this power. And it is through such bold moves towards urban renaissance that we create the opportunities to make a better city.

The royal parks and palaces play a vital role in the working of London. They highlight the difference between the City of Westminster and the City of London: the seat of government and monarchy on the one hand, and the seat of commerce on the other. These two sectors are as contrasting in urban plan as they are in function. Westminster evolved in an extraordinarily suburban, almost rural manner, while the City has its roots in the Roman fortified citadel. Together, they form the rather split personality that is the metropolis of London.

The City of London is a typologically true European town. Roman in origin, it is planned around dense, gridded street patterns, a wall, gated entries and a high street. In the way that the Romans prescribed for their military purposes, the City is 20 minutes' walk from one side to the other. A truly urban form, its compact size made it ideal for banking purposes in the nineteenth and twentieth centuries, and practical for anti-terrorist barricades in the late twentieth and early twenty-first century.

Next to this tight form is the open, non-urban territory of the West End, which is based on the random placing of four palaces (Buckingham, St James's, Kensington and Westminster) and six royal parks (Kensington Gardens, Hyde Park, Green Park, Buckingham Palace, St James's Park and Regent's Park). The royal palaces and their parks were originally built as anti-urban set pieces: they are great country houses set in rural parkland, intended as hunting grounds. Over the years, the parks have evolved and have become enmeshed and assimilated in the dense urban fabric. This shift occurred for two reasons: firstly, London expanded and enveloped the parks, and, secondly, the monarchy has diminished and a democratic modern state has gradually grown in its place. Assimilating the royal parks into the urban plan was a significant part of the legacy of John Nash, under the championship of the Prince Regent. Nash's urban plans capitalised on this encroachment, interweaving London's public areas within what was then the exclusive settings of the royal parks.

Of these two arenas of power, it is the City of Westminster that has the true British character – after all, it is the seat of the government and monarchy. By some strange quirk of fate, the City of London has become purely a place of trade and commerce. As a specialised trading quarter, it lacks the diversity and heterogeneity of other urban districts. As a result, the integration of the City of Westminster and the City of London is still waiting to happen. The fusion of the two places cannot occur unless the City's view of itself shifts from being a purely trading centre to existing as part of London proper.

What are we left with today? In essence, the royal palaces and their parklands are the only public realm that we have in London. Far from being something that we are ashamed of, they present an opportunity for a glorious public realm. My desire is to see their full integration into the fabric of London in a positive, creative and visionary way. We need to carry on Nash's work to integrate the royal palaces and their parklands, and we need to address the problem of the urban fabric between and beyond them. The result would be a London in which the parks, palaces and city fabric are planned as one. Currently, the parks are walled off from the palaces, the palaces are privatised and the surrounding urban fabric has problems of access and connectivity to the parks. The design implication is that the parks are no more than largesse from royalty – a place where the public are occasionally allowed to walk.

## The London of Wren and Nash

The unique disconnection between the West End and the City is one reason for the shape of London today. The other is the legacy handed down to us by Wren (in paper form) and Nash. These two great urban architects offered contrasting approaches to town planning in Britain. After the Great Fire, Wren tried to impose on the City an axial arrangement of grand boulevards, as found in the classically planned cities of Paris, Rome and Berlin. His plans failed because of the vested interest in privately owned, fragmented plots of land.

Why did Nash succeed where Wren failed? Nash enjoyed two great advantages over Wren. The first is that he was building in the West End where there was less private and more public ownership, albeit through the monarch. This resulted in large centralised holdings of land – a simpler form of land ownership than Wren had to contend with in the City. His second advantage was his partnership with landscape gardener Humphry Repton. Together, they evolved an approach to town planning based on British landscape design. The result is the development of the 'picturesque' approach to city planning, which was first outlined in Repton's Red Book. Repton showed that the best landscape improvement schemes for the aristocracy's country estates adapted the garden design around the natural landscape of woodlands, lakes and hills. This picturesque handling contradicted the French convention, which completely reworked the landscape into a purely man-made and symmetrical environment of great boulevards and axes. It was seized on by Nash, who applied it brilliantly to town planning. The result is typified by Trafalgar Square, Regent Street and Regent's Park.

What can we learn from Nash today? Let us explore Buckingham Palace as a case study. The building has not changed since Edward VII's time, when the palace was a symbol of empire. For all its wedding cake finery, it is not the actual building that landmarks the site of national importance. The signifier is the urban setting: the sweeping circle (sadly a roundabout) around Victoria monument, the gilded gates and the powerful juxtaposition of travelling from the imperialist monument that is Buckingham Palace to Hyde Park's slice of English countryside. Yet this setting is a piece of great urban theatre that is being played out without the full involvement of the British public. The whole set piece must be arranged to work better: catering for pedestrians above cars. Compare its present bleakness to Europe's wonderful paved squares and open spaces.

The palace itself needs to be opened up and transformed from its current heavy, impermeable state. The social and political conditions that created the linked parks and palaces no longer prevail. Institutions are now required to be civic-minded and accountable. Somerset House – once a forbidding complex of government offices and now a wonderful public space – is a great example of this.

## Who owns Buckingham Palace?

Ambivalence about the role of the royal family versus the rights of the public means that neither side gets the full benefit of these urban masterpieces. Buckingham Palace and its park are part of a collection of urban forms that distinguish London from other cities; in world terms they are truly unique. No other city has its great palaces linked to parkland in this way and on this scale. Yet while the royal family barricade their gardens behind high walls, the experience for all is hesitatingly and incompletely revealed – the opposite intention of the original designs. The walls around Buckingham Palace's gardens depress the urban scene for over a mile of central London. They are the epitome of bad neighbourliness and characterise the palace as a series of signs that say 'Keep Out'.

We need to prick the defensive bubble and once again open up the palace and its park to the public gaze. My proposal is to create a radical new physical and emotional relationship between the palace and the people. The challenge is to humanise the area in front of the palace in order to create a more open connection between it and the building. Perforating the palace's screen wall with arches or columns would expose the hidden courtyard, and link it up with the public space in front of the palace. This extremely simple gesture would create a grand processional route. Buckingham Palace's facade would become a gateway, as opposed to a barrier. The new square would become the first in a sequence of spaces that would allow people to walk down the Mall, through the square, through the old Nash courtyard, and then into the splendid gardens of Buckingham Palace beyond. Like any owner of a great country house, the Queen could continue to live in private quarters with all the levels of security that she presently enjoys.

My next set of urban improvements would involve perforating Buckingham Palace's garden walls with inset railings (like the enclosures around Brompton Cemetery) and gates, which would be just as secure as the present wall. Buckingham Palace and its grounds would then be integrated with the rest of central London and open for all to walk through. I would like to see a great promenade from the Mall, up Constitution Hill, across Hyde Park Corner, through the Wellington Arch and Decimus Burton's screen and along Rotten Row to Kensington Palace. This route could be enlivened by events, pavilions, cafés and restaurants – similar to those found in Kew Gardens. With the walls encircling the palace gardens removed, Buckingham, St James's and Kensington Palaces would be 80 per cent open to the public, allowing a flourish of exhibitions, galleries, museums, and concerts in the palaces themselves.

### Urban design and governance

These plans would reintegrate large areas of London, extending and building on original designs. It is only through such brave physical changes that London can develop to embrace the needs of the new century. We must continue Nash's approach to town planning in order that the parks and palaces successfully evolve into vibrant quarters of the city.

This leads on to the often neglected argument for the urban design of capital cities as a positive expression of governance. Great capital cities use architecture and urban design to imply a strong organisational, governmental base for the city plan itself. This is self-evident in completely new cities such as Canberra, Washington or Brasilia – capital cities that are invented as capital cities. Contrastingly, in historical cities such as Paris, Beijing, Berlin or Edinburgh, the seat of government evolved at the same time as the city itself. In Paris, the great axis running from the old political centre of Versailles, through the Champs Élysées to the Louvre is part of the city's urban identity. Similarly, the great axis and walls are part of the city plan of Beijing; and in Edinburgh, the castle, Royal Mile and Holyrood Palace are part of the city itself.

In London's West End – the heart of empire as it was called 100 years ago – the relationship between Buckingham Palace, Parliament Square and Trafalgar Square is the key to understanding the expression of governance. Yet this layout is also an extraordinary misrepresentation. Buckingham Palace is the grandest of all the buildings. Yet the elected head of state – the prime minister – lives in a little terraced house to the side of Parliament Square.

The implications of these three spaces – Buckingham Palace, Parliament Square and Trafalgar Square – are intriguing. Parliament Square, in the form of Westminster Abbey, symbolises the religious centre, while the Palace of Westminster symbolises the parliamentary centre. This is Government and Church united. Trafalgar Square – another unsatisfactory public space – is used for strangely controlled protests and gatherings. The third space is in front of Buckingham Palace, which is where we gather to celebrate events of national importance: marriages, deaths, wartime victories and great national successes.

To paraphrase Winston Churchill, we form our places and our places form us. This is what fascinates me about Buckingham Palace and its role in misrepresenting the structure of government that we have today. When the US President wishes to make a declaration, he is conspicuously seen against the backdrop of the White House, driving through the great streets of Washington to the Capitol buildings. The journey evidences a clear statement about the balance of power between the President, Congress and Senate.

By contrast, the urban form of London obscures the clarity of democratic government. If we do indeed make our places and our places make us, then we have to question how they are now remaking us. With humility, collaboration and confidence, architects must be actively involved in this debate. It is our responsibility to ensure that our places are making us what we want to be.

*Sir Terry Farrell is an award-winning architect and urban designer. His firm's prominent masterplans include Embankment Place in London, the Quayside in Newcastle upon Tyne and the waterfront in Hull.*

# Part 4

Happy and glorious

# Families valued

Do we have a psychological need for the monarchy?

## Raj Persaud

One peculiar characteristic of our age is that every day someone somewhere appears to be apologising publicly for something. Recent high-profile repentances include: regrets for ignoring atrocities committed in the Second World War; for experiments performed on minorities; for apartheid; for biting an opponent in a prize fight; for trying to bury bad news; and for having an inappropriate relationship with a White House intern. Whomever these apologies might be immediately directed towards, it is clear they are really for public consumption. They are intended to repair a tarnished image, through what the sociologist Erving Goffman termed 'face-work': a form of persuasive discourse designed to restore a damaged reputation.

Reputation is ever more important in a world where what you know of others is rarely determined by direct personal contact. Whenever our image is at risk, face-work becomes a necessary and vital strategy. Recent psychological research has found face-work to be a universal behaviour – not only among individuals, but also leaders, corporations and celebrities. All engage in a discourse of image restoration when their reputation is threatened.

It follows that if there are people who never do face-work, this speaks volumes about the power relationship between them and their audience. It is perhaps the ultimate marker of total dominance when face-work is not necessary between one party and another. One can still conceive that face-work may be necessary between a boss and a worker, but not perhaps between a master and a slave.

Therefore it is psychologically interesting that a notable exception to the universal use of face-work is the British royal family. In the last few centuries, the royal family has only appeared to do face-work on two occasions: the first being King Edward VIII's apology following his abdication; the second being the Queen's address to the nation the evening before Princess Diana's funeral.

Following Diana's death, the Queen was rebuked by the media for failing to acknowledge her subjects' overwhelming grief. As the *Independent* put it at the time, 'if only the Royals dared weep with the people.' This rapidly turned into a public relations nightmare for the monarchy, and the ferocity of the attacks forced the Queen to respond. In a significant break with royal protocol, the Queen ordered the Royal Standard to fly at half-mast during Diana's funeral. Even more remarkable was the Queen's address to the British public the evening before. In a normal year, the Queen makes only two scheduled public addresses – at Christmas and at the State Opening of Parliament. In the previous 45 years of her reign, she had made only one other unscheduled public address.

That speech marked a pivotal moment in the nation's relationship with the monarchy. For the first time, it became clear that the royal family needs to be concerned with public relations, just like any modern government or corporation. The future of the royal brand relies far more on how it is managed than on its actual practical usefulness. The royal family may shudder at the thought of engaging in face-work and 'brand management', but it will have to learn fast. In an age of consumerism, even royalty has 'customers' that it needs to care for. In the modern age, if you sit on a throne, you need to be aware of who put you there, and who can make your life so uncomfortable that you prefer to get off.

The more republican newspapers routinely try to write off the monarchy. But the evidence from opinion polls suggests otherwise. MORI, the polling organisation, has been asking the

British public what they think of the monarchy for decades, and has not detected much of a change in public opinion. The usual question MORI asks is: 'On balance, do you think Britain would be better off or worse off if the monarchy was abolished, or do you think it would make no difference?' In April 1984, only 5 per cent of the public thought the country would be better off, while 77 per cent believed it would be worse off. In the year 2000, when MORI asked 'If there were a referendum on the issue, would you favour Britain becoming a republic or remaining a monarchy?' 19 per cent favoured a republic, while an overwhelming 70 per cent preferred Britain to remain a monarchy. Levels of support have risen even higher in the wake of the Queen Mother's death.

Yet often what people say to someone wielding a clipboard is not an accurate measure of real sentiment. Psychologists theorise that there might be a basic human need for an 'upwardly directed' relationship in which a superior figure is looked up to. This could explain the universality of God figures in cultures around the world, perhaps filling a need created by the earlier child–parent relationship. Our modern require-ments, perhaps influenced by democracy, appear more com-plicated, in that we feel a need to look up to someone but also to identify with them in some way – to feel they share some common bond with us. If a person can capture this compli-cated mix, they create an especially emotive relationship with the public.

### Emotional identification

The death of the Princess of Wales is arguably the event that has had the widest effect on public emotions in recent years. Some psychotherapists at the time described the huge communal outpouring of grief as 'hysterical'. Research published recently by the University of Oxford's Centre for Suicide Research reveals a massive rise in suicides in England and Wales following Diana's death.[1] The researchers analysed the number of suicides in England and Wales, and found an overall increase of 17 per cent in the month afterwards. Even more startling was the discovery that the impact was greatest on women, particularly women closest in age to Diana herself,

1 Available at www.psy-chiatry.ox.ac.uk/csr.

who died aged 37. The rate of suicide among women aged 25–44 increased by over 45 per cent in the month after Diana's death. This suggests an identification factor at work: the people who most identified with the Princess were most affected by her death. Particularly intriguing was the research finding that there was no increase in suicides among those already known to mental health professionals. This suggests that many of those who were fundamentally affected by Diana's death were not those who would normally be classified as 'vulnerable'.

Traditionally psychiatrists have seen suicide as a response to the breakdown of an important relationship in a person's life, but clearly the vast majority of people who committed suicide or self-harmed (rates of self-harm went up 65 per cent in women during the week following Diana's death) had never met Diana. Perhaps this confirms that we are entering a new age of celebrity, where many of us form relationships with public figures which have just as much significance for our personal lives as those with the people we actually meet. Identification with Diana might have been particularly strong for women of her age because she seemed to suffer the problems typical of the modern young woman: issues of body preoccupation and obsessive dieting; confusion over career goals; relationship difficulties; and a lack of support from previous generations of female relatives.

The example of Diana contrasts with the period immediately following President Kennedy's assassination, when the national suicide rate in the USA temporarily declined. The theory advocated then was that the nation uniting in mourning meant that people felt more connected with each other and their community, so reducing isolation and loneliness. Although Diana's death and funeral were accompanied by astonishing scenes of shared grieving, it appears that the crowds did not succeed in making us feel closer to each other in quite the same way.

### A campaigning family?
The royal family might be able to learn something from this research. If they want to preserve the public's high esteem and

ensure that Britain never becomes a republic, it could be argued that they have to become a group with which the ordinary person can more easily identify. This seems a tall order given the obvious barriers of wealth and privilege. Members of the royal family may be uncomfortable with this cynical view of a possible role, but it is clear that they themselves are groping for a part to play in the nation's life.

A brand manager might look at this recent history and make a radical recommendation: that the royals should become a campaigning family – more obviously fighting for their subjects than they do now. Some of the causes Diana picked, like landmine clearance, may have provided great picture opportunities, but a refocused royal family would have to concentrate on the needy nearer home. Charles has already stirred things up with his interest in alternative medicine, organic food and architecture – but how many of these are the daily concerns of the vast majority of his future subjects?

There are obvious problems with this strategy. An actively campaigning family is likely to end up in conflict with vested interests, such as big business, the government and the professions. But a popular and a populist royal family could ride on a wave of public support so strong that few would want to challenge them. With the decline of the unions and proper investigative journalism, perhaps the royal family could step into the gap and expose the hidden conditions that so many of their subjects endure?

Ironically, the real danger to any new strategy comes from the royals' immense wealth – for if they are to start displaying an increased concern for their subjects, the inevitable cry will rise up asking why they don't do something about it themselves, with their resources? It is likely that they will, as one of the wealthiest families in the country, need to do a bit more than pose for pictures if they want to appear genuinely interested in suffering or injustice. So maybe the royals will have to give some of their wealth away, rather as Bill Gates and other modern philanthropists have done?

Some will question whether the royals really have to do so much to obtain respect from their subjects – after all, are we not in an age where many achieve celebrity and adulation for doing very little? The psychological advantage of not doing very much is that it allows the public to project their own fantasies on to you without reality having to intervene. But the downside of this approach is that the press needs a never-ending supply of new pictures, and you end up competing with *Pop Idol* and *Big Brother*. Not exactly a sustainable strategy for the future of the monarchy.

*Dr Raj Persaud is a Consultant Psychiatrist and Senior Lecturer at the Maudsley Hospital and Institute of Psychiatry in London.*

# Courting fame

The monarchy and celebrity culture

**Chris Rojek**

Life for your average monarch used to be a lot more straight-forward. By dint of bloodline, the monarch was the ultimate ascribed celebrity in society. Appointed by divine right, the monarch's function was to rule. The sanctions and opinions of the populace were significant but seldom of pressing moment, and the monarch was never placed under the microscope of the media or public opinion. Indeed the principal rituals and symbols of monarchy were all designed to emphasise the immemorial remoteness of the monarch from ordinary men and women.

Celebrity status comes in two forms: ascribed and achieved. Ascribed celebrity concerns lineage: status typically follows from bloodline. The celebrity of Caroline Kennedy or Prince William stems from their line of biological descent. It is why kings and queens in earlier social formations commanded automatic respect and veneration. Individuals may add to or subtract from their ascribed status by virtue of their voluntary actions, but the foundation of their ascribed celebrity is prede-termined.

In contrast, achieved celebrity derives from the perceived accomplishments of the individual in open competition. For example, Brad Pitt, Damien Hirst, Michael Jordan, Darcy Bussell, David Beckham, Lennox Lewis, Pete Sampras, Venus and Serena Williams, and Monica Seles are celebrities by reason of their artistic or sporting achievements. In the public realm they are recognised as individuals who possess rare talents or skills.

## The changing nature of royal celebrity

Three tendencies have complicated this picture. First, power has gradually shifted from the monarch, initially to the court, but with the rise of democracy, to the electorate and their representatives. Of course, the Queen retains significant political and legal power. But for all practical intents and purposes the exercise of this power is a matter for government ministers who are accountable to the electorate. The Queen's role is overwhelmingly symbolic, even if the question of what the monarch symbolises has become somewhat harder to resolve.

Second, mass communications have penetrated the veil of privacy that once separated the monarch from the public. It is no longer sufficient for the monarch to rule by means of what one might call 'courtly ventriloquism', whereby the monarch's beliefs, values and intentions are conveyed to the populace through intermediaries. Today, the monarch must engage directly with the public through the media. We now think of this in terms of the Diana effect. Throughout the difficulties of her marriage, the Princess beat the royal family at their own game by using the media to shift public opinion in her favour. The Queen's decision to make a live broadcast to the nation after Diana's death was a tacit admission that royalty no longer possessed the option to remain aloof.

Third, the rise of *achieved* celebrity culture has challenged the ascendancy of ascribed celebrity. We now live in an age dominated by achieved celebrities. David Beckham, Robbie Williams, Naomi Campbell and Kate Winslet command public attention by virtue of their actions rather than their bloodline. Moreover, this list of *British* achieved celebrities instantly appears deficient because it misses one of the central aspects of achieved celebrity today: globalisation. Achieved celebrities spring from the ranks of ordinary people, but their spectacular upward mobility elevates them to a pre-eminent position in global culture. Ascribed celebrities such as Prince William and

Prince Harry continue to command a generous measure of public attention. But they do so in a celebrity market place dominated by a galaxy of achieved celebrities like the model Giselle Bundchen, Johnny Depp, Venus Williams and Mel Gibson. In democratic societies, where the story of the people has largely replaced the story of the monarchy as the central narrative of history, the dynamics of achieved celebrity appear more relevant.

## Edward and Margaret

To some extent, British royalty has long understood the shifting balance of power between ascribed and achieved celebrity. For example, in the 1920s and 1930s, Edward VIII cultivated his reputation for communicating with ordinary people. This was in sharp contrast to the regal austerity maintained by his parents, George V and Queen Mary. But like Diana after him, Edward had an unerring habit of igniting controversy. For example, his donation of ten pounds to a relief fund set up for miners after the General Strike of 1926 and his comments about the evil of unemployment enraged the establishment. He became marked as a loose cannon, and his liaison with Wallis Simpson, and subsequent abdication, appeared to confirm this opinion. George VI's and Elizabeth II's reversion to a more formal style of rule can certainly be interpreted as a reaction to Edward's perceived waywardness.

Yet to some degree, Princess Margaret, especially in her twenties, carried on many aspects of Edward's legacy. In her youth, she had a notorious relationship with a married commoner, Group Captain Peter Townsend. She later married the society photographer Anthony Armstrong-Jones and enthusiastically plunged into the world of 1960s celebrity, befriending the actor Peter Sellers, the novelist Robin Douglas-Home and John Bindon, a tough-guy with links to the London underworld. After her relationship with Armstrong-Jones disintegrated, she embarked on a highly public affair with Roddy Llewellyn. However, although Margaret associated with achieved celebrities, it was never on the basis of equality. After her relationship with Llewellyn ended, there was no real comparison between her treatment at the hands of the media and the victimisation of a film star or pop idol of the day. She was always a royal, unalterably distinct from other people.

In this respect, Diana, Princess of Wales, represented a genuine turning point in the relationship between monarchy and achieved celebrity. Only a few weeks before her death, she was filmed comforting a tearful Elton John at Gianni Versace's funeral. It was an embrace between two victims of fame who, despite all of their wealth and prestige, were understood to walk a fine line between public acclaim and private abjection. Symbolically, it was a moment when ascribed and achieved celebrity came together.

Diana adopted the wardrobe, global outlook and perform-ance rituals of achieved celebrity culture. Her high-profile campaigns for AIDS victims, the homeless, victims of domestic violence and against the international trade in landmines created the public perception of an active citizen rather than a remote royal. After the collapse of her marriage, her candid tele-vision and press interviews expressed the vulnerabilities of being in the limelight. It is true that as a member of the aris-tocracy, she inherited many of the prestige attributes of ascribed status. Perhaps the most important was that the royal family automatically considered her to be part of the social stratum worthy of providing a suitable partner for the future king of England. Be that as it may, the travails of her marriage and the apparent indifference of the Windsors to her distress isolated her from the royal establishment. Yet Diana declined to adopt a discreet approach to her plight and eventually appealed directly to the public through the media. Unlike Edward VIII, who reluctantly accepted exile, she increased her independence and prominence in British life. Assiduously and pointedly, she cultivated a different way of being royal that was clearly intended to shape the outlook of her sons, William and Harry.

## Lifestyles of the rich and famous

When achieved celebrities suffer career strain, they frequently employ the TV chat show and the tabloid press in pursuit of public redemption. Diana's use of the media after the collapse of her marriage was more restrained, but it adopted the same techniques of disclosing private traumas to camera in return for public sympathy and compassion. Her public appearances, her film star wardrobe, and her adoption of public causes, were increasingly guided by the advice of public relations experts. These rituals of glamorous engagement with the media, and the active courting of not merely public approval but idolatry, are the standard practices of Hollywood publicists. Diana employed them to great effect.

For achieved celebrities, the split between the private self and the public face is often the source of acute anxiety. The public face is continually engaged in performance, pandering to media expectations and gingerly anticipating changes in the public mood. Achieved celebrities often complain that the performance rituals of the public face engulf the sense of a private self, producing a great deal of emotional distress. Certainly, achieved celebrities suffer higher-than-average rates of divorce, mental illness and premature death. Diana's eating disorders were symptoms of the self-destructive behaviour that often accompanies achieved celebrity. Her untimely death places her in the pantheon of achieved celebrities – Marilyn Monroe, Judy Garland, John Lennon and Kurt Cobain – who are at some level regarded as martyrs to the demands of the media and an insatiable public.

## Pop idols and pin-ups

Prince Charles's approach to achieved celebrity has always been more diffident. One senses that he was embarrassed by Diana's antics in cultivating film stars and pop idols. Outwardly, he seems more comfortable with the protocols of ascribed celebrity. He prefers hunting, farming and polo to movie premières, pop concerts and television studios. Although he occasionally makes controversial statements about architecture and the environment, he is a reserved character, given to the strong sense of duty that characterised the public role of his parents and grandparents. His work with the Prince's Trust has made a steady and imaginative contribution to social entrepreneurship in Britain, but it has never attained the status of a national *cause célèbre* that Diana achieved with her involvement in the anti-landmines campaign.

The opportunities for modernisation of the monarchy rest in

Charles's hands, but his most important asset is undoubtedly Prince William. Charismatic, photogenic and, in the public mind, the fullest embodiment of Diana's legacy, William is the key to the future of the monarchy. If the primary function of the monarch today is symbolic, it will be up to Charles, William and their advisers to construct a symbol that can embrace a multicultural Britain, increasingly bound to Europe.

Redoubling the regal status of ascribed celebrity is no option at all. Over time, the balance of power between the monarch and society has shifted decisively and irrevocably in favour of the people. The monarch can no longer be completely above the people, since this would be perceived as haughty, imperious and out of touch. The most favourable option is to be *for* the people by engaging in deserving causes and acting as a tribune for the public interest. To some extent, Charles has already adopted this role through his interventions on the environment, public architecture and unemployment. But it will be left to William to play an enlarged role by engaging more wholeheartedly with business, education, the media and the arts.

Inevitably, this points to greater convergence with the world of achieved celebrity, where, culturally speaking, the action is now located. Monarchs can never be meritocrats since their status ultimately derives from the ascription of bloodline. But they can be held in public esteem, standing for the people rather than for the interests of business or government. In societies that in all other salient respects purport to be democracies, this is the best rebuke to republicanism.

*Chris Rojek is Professor of Sociology and Culture at Nottingham Trent University. His most recent books are* Celebrity *(2001) and* Stuart Hall *(2002).*

# Tantrums and tiaras

How the monarchy accessorised fashion

**Jess Cartner-Morley**

On the opening night of the Victoria & Albert Museum's exhibition of some of the world's most famous and valuable tiaras in March 2002, a minor incident took place between Camilla Parker Bowles and the Duchess of Devonshire. The Duchess, who had loaned a tiara to the exhibition, was reported to be furious that Mrs Parker Bowles was singled out for a private tour of the glittering exhibits. 'I suppose she is surveying her kingdom,' the Duchess is alleged to have said.

Apocryphal or not, the story was seized on by the media long starved of court scandal of such glamorous complexion. The emotive symbolism of the tiara exhibition reminds us not only of a time when fashion was set by the royal court – but that the legacy of monarchism retains an influence on fashion today.

Tiaras make a good starting point for a look at monarchy and fashion. Not technically a royal item – legend has it that ivy wreaths were first worn by the Greek god Dionysus and his followers, and humble versions known as *kokoshnik* were once popular among Russian peasants – they are nonetheless as closely allied with royalty, in the public imagination, as palaces. No little girl's 'princess' fancy dress costume would be complete without one.

Now, however, they are enjoying a renaissance as a fashion item. The age-old tradition of a woman wearing a tiara on her wedding day has become commonplace through all strata of society, with cheap rhinestone or mother-of-pearl tiaras sold in every bridal store. Among the well-to-do, 'status' tiaras have become a key part of glamorous weddings. For her wedding in a Scottish castle, Madonna's 'something borrowed' was a nineteenth-century 78-carat diamond tiara in a conventional floral garland style, loaned for the day by royal jewellers Asprey & Garrard.

Many of the new generation of tiara wearers are unbothered by the niceties of etiquette. Traditionally, only married women wore tiaras, for instance, and to wear one in a hotel was a *faux pas*. Now tiaras are worn by teenage clubbers: the stones may be paste, but the link to a princess fantasy lends ample sparkle. What's more, young women can take a pick'n'mix approach to the princess look, wearing their tiaras with jeans or miniskirts.

The famously *outré* singer Courtney Love subverted the connotations of the tiara by teaming it with smudged red lipstick and garishly bleached hair. Decades before, punk subculture already had a complex fascination with monarchy and its trappings; indeed, the brightly coloured spikes of the Mohican and related punk haircuts mirrored, in a fashion, the Queen's own headgear. And it was a logical progression for Vivienne Westwood to later declare herself more interested, as a designer, in high culture than street culture. Today, Westwood can sometimes be seen bicycling through London wearing a Neapolitan coral tiara from the 1870s.

Recently, peacockish elements of the male royal wardrobe have emerged as elements of the images of rap stars such as Puff Daddy – and spoof stars such as Sacha Baron Cohen's comic creation, Ali G. Puff Daddy's gold jewellery is ostentatiously displayed in ceremonial fashion. The poses which he and fellow rappers assume for publicity shots and videos, ceremonially surrounded by sports cars, bottles of champagne and women in bikinis, may seem unremittingly contemporary in their vulgarity. However, they have forebears, of a sort, in traditional portraits of landowners posing proudly with their horses and finely attired wives, ancestral homes painstakingly painted in behind.

Moreover, the outsize silhouette favoured by rap artists –

designed to enable, or suggest, the carrying of weapons beneath – wittingly or unwittingly lends a royal air. In Puff Daddy's penchant for overly large coats of white fur, worn over pinstripe suits or leather jackets even in summer, we find a reminder of the costumes worn by Byzantine emperors when they wanted to impress. For example, in the year 325, Emperor Constantine met with the Nicaean Council to attempt to quell growing unrest. He wore, it is recorded, gold-embroidered, jewel-encrusted purple robes, high-heeled red buskins, and a spiked tiara.[1]

## The aesthetics of monarchy

Royal aesthetics have always been about wealth, status and visibility. Tiaras have links with notions of romantic love: the wearing of one on a wedding day is supposed to symbolise the crowning of love over innocence. But in a royal wedding, the more humble stones which symbolise love – pearls and turquoise – are less favoured than diamonds. The 14th Earl of Strathmore was following a long royal tradition when he gave his daughter, Lady Elizabeth Bowes-Lyon (later the Queen Mother), a tiara of rose-cut diamonds on her marriage to the Duke of York. Diamonds may represent eternity and beauty, but they also stand for wealth and power.

A true tiara is a complete circle, like a crown. (Anything else, strictly speaking, is a diadem.) Often, tiaras are designed in a 'spiked' setting similar to a traditional crown. This design has the effect of making the wearer's status evident, even when glimpsed, from any angle and from some distance. What's more, a tiara, like a crown – and indeed like the ruffs favoured by gentlemen and women of the sixteenth century – forces the wearer to hold his or her head high, and so give the impression of aristocratic hauteur.

When made of diamonds or pearls, a tiara gives the wearer a halo effect: a ring of divine beauty. Little wonder it was so long popular among royal families keen to demarcate their special status. But the flamboyant design and literally unforgettable beauty of many royal tiaras – the vast Siberian amethysts of the Russian gems, the gobstopper-sized emeralds of the French crown jewels, the dazzling sunburst diamond tiara which

1 B Cosgrave, *Costume and Fashion: a complete history* (London: Hamlyn, 2000).

Queen Victoria wore on her first visit to the opera – also served a more prosaic purpose. In the days before photographs, few subjects had much notion of their monarch's physical appearance; what better way to indelibly mark your image on the public memory than through fantastical jewels? The Duchess of Devonshire recently recalled,

> When I was a young woman in the 1930s, one's tiara was a kind of identity card. The face underneath was known by the helmet of diamonds, rubies, emeralds, sapphires and pearls glittering on her head: harsh, spiky and upstanding, or rounded in the shapes of flowers or leaves; tall like a nursery fender, or a humbler circlet threaded through the Marcel waves of the hair. It was like recognising people in a country crowd by their dogs. We would have been very muddled if there had been a general swap around and the Duchess of Northumberland wore Lady Astor's, and Lady Londonderry turned up in one of the Duchess of Buccleuch's.[2]

**Monarchy and the exercise of aesthetic power**

For royalty, jewellery takes precedence over clothes. Queen Elizabeth II instinctively knew this when faced with a last-minute wardrobe crisis before a state banquet she was giving for the Reagans in 1983. When her couturier, Hardy Amies, presented her with the dress he had designed for the occasion, it was found that the dramatic bows on the shoulders did not work with the earrings and tiara she planned to wear. Amies was distraught. 'Oh, don't go on about it,' she told him. 'I think it's a very pretty dress and I'm going to like it. Just take the bows off.'[3]

Queen Elizabeth the Queen Mother also used jewellery to stake her position. The demure pearls which were a lifelong favourite were viewed, early in her marriage, in stark contrast to Wallis Simpson's glittering panther brooches. This wholesome image worked in her favour when the abdication of Edward VIII thrust her into the limelight. But with

**2** *Sunday Telegraph*, 17 Mar 2002.
**3** S Bradford, *Elizabeth: a biography of Her Majesty the Queen* (London: Penguin, 1996).

the proliferation of photography, the Queen Mother was forced to pay closer attention to all her clothes. She developed a highly distinctive look, a penchant for pastels which contributed to the public's sentimental image of her. For 50 years, from the death of George VI in 1952 to her own death in 2002, her style changed little. In this, she came to represent an image of safe constancy in contrast to the increasingly lurid lives of her grandchildren.

## Monarch as fashion icon

But it was the Queen Mother's granddaughter-in-law, Diana, who became the royal family's only twentieth-century style icon. Diana, who began straightforwardly enough as a young bride whose haircut and wedding dress spawned a thousand suburban copies, but who was rather looked down upon by the world of high fashion, metamorphosed into someone closely entwined with the fashion industry.

In contrast to the figure of the Queen Mother, which Clementine Churchill once compared to 'a plump turtledove', Diana became model-thin; 'becoming' pastels were swapped for dramatic black and chic beige. Towards the end of her life, she was a *Vogue* cover girl courted by designers around the world. But the fact that it had been Diana who changed to meet the requirements of fashion, rather than the other way around, hinted at the changing power dynamics of monarchy and the worlds of style and celebrity.

Diana's willingness to play the fashion icon stemmed, perhaps, from her understanding of the limitations of her role in the royal family. Like many wives before her, she had all the beauty, but none of the power. The revealing black dress which she wore, famously, to a gala at the Serpentine Gallery the night that Prince Charles admitted in a television interview to having committed adultery suggested that she saw her image as her most potent weapon in her public and private struggles.

The aesthetics of monarchy have been dispersed and subverted by a changing social structure. Once, monarchs could have divided threats to their position into those who had breeding but no money, and those who had wealth but no glamour. Huge diamonds and white furs quite clearly denote both. Such demarcations seem archaic now. And it is often the people with both money and glamour but from very far outside the royal circle – Madonna, or Puff Daddy – who most boldly claim the aesthetics of royalty as their own.

Snobbery, too, has moved on. Who designed an item now holds more cachet than whose bank vault it came from. As the pace of commercial fashion has speeded up, that of court fashion, which once had courtiers panting to keep up with the latest fad, has ground almost to a halt. Where royal influences emerge, they are historical rather than contemporary. The peacockish robes of male rap stars have more in common with the garb of Henry VIII than with that of Prince Charles.

Royal influences in contemporary fashion are symptoms not of a forelock-tugging emulation but of a cheerfully insubordinate attitude to the glitz and glamour that was once out of reach of ordinary people. In James Hayllar's 1863 painting, *Going to Court*, two women, probably a mother and daughter, are seen in their carriage on their way to court for presentation to the sovereign. They are wearing delicate white gowns with bare shoulders, pearl necklaces, feather fans, silk gloves and diamond tiaras. Onlookers can be seen peering in through the window, huddled beneath their umbrellas and heavy coats. Once, it seems, the court circle shone, and the rest were dowdy. On this, however, the monarchy can no longer rely.

*Jess Cartner-Morley is fashion editor of* The Guardian

# Redeemed characters

How the nation views the monarchy as soap opera

**John Yorke**

If there is one story that drives soap opera, it's redemption. Increasingly it is a theme that drives that other national saga, 'The Windsors' too. I have no idea whether this is a conscious decision, but to me as the producer of another of the nation's favourite soaps, it appears as if the royal script editors are putting the redemption theme at the heart of their PR strategy. If it is deliberate, they are using a powerful narrative technique that connects with people at a deep emotional level.

The stories we tell in soaps are based on old fairy tales with a moral subtext, and that is true of the cast of royals too. Whatever the reality, the media have accorded them symbolic roles – the matriarch and the patriarch, the rogue son and the Cinderella princess. The royals have been thrust into roles created for them, partly by the media but also by centuries of storytelling.

So in a way, just as on *EastEnders* we create a storyline for our characters, the media – conscious of a need deep within us all – are creating a set of characters and a storyline for the royal family to play out. Our appetite for 'good' royals and 'bad' royals appears to be insatiable; and within those two polarities lies the most exciting drama of all – the character journey from bad to good and its reverse, the fall from grace. Of the former, Camilla is perhaps the classic example; of the latter we need look no further than the Duke and Duchess of Wessex.

Whatever the realities of their situation – and we can be sure that they're considerably more complex than we allow – the classical demands of narrative force them into simple, straightforward character arcs.

So, if Prince Edward and Sophie currently occupy pride of place in the pantheon of soap 'badness', is it actually possible to redeem them? In narrative terms the early signs are good. By casting off their black cloaks (TV producer and PR guru respectively) and acceding to a sense of duty, they have already placed their first foot on the ladder of redemption. They have now embarked on a period of penance and good works – the royal equivalent of sackcloth and ashes. In the months and years to come, they will have to open a lot of school sports centres and eat a lot of rubber chicken – but if they stick assiduously to the path of righteousness, there seems no reason why they should not once again be allowed to embrace the pageantry that is the Duke's birthright. In classical narratives, the birth of a child would represent a symbol of renewal, and it may be through that route that Edward and Sophie eventually win back the affections of the British public.

It may seem like a cliché, but audiences really do want a happy ending, just as much as they wish to see sinners repent, and if Edward and Sophie weren't already married (real life has a habit of messing up conventional narratives) a scriptwriter would insist on this perfect symbolic act for their final reacceptance into the affections of the British public. This hunger for narrative closure is nowhere more readily illustrated than in the case of 'Camilla'.

### Camilla's happy ending

From a script-editing perspective the story of 'Camilla' has been handled extremely well; all that remains as we enter the third act is to write the happy ending. If the wedding provides this perfect sense of closure, what's important about it is not so much the ceremony itself, but the narrative arc that leads up to it. For above all weddings need to be *earned*; and it is here that Camilla's story may prove to be most successful.

Rule one of soap structure dictates that central characters have to make sacrifices and overcome obstacles to prove they are worthy of eternal happiness. What's more – and in an interesting twist that may be peculiar to soap – they should be seen to overcome these tests without complaint. Characters who feel sorry for themselves almost never win the public's affection. Not only must they suffer, but it is important that they suffer with dignity and heroic stoicism. As the royals never comment on their own personal travails, they actually lend themselves perfectly to these preanointed parts – and Camilla, who has steadfastly stood by her love through thick and thin, has played hers most perfectly of all.

So if we accept that we all respond to narrative on a deeply emotional level, that we long for a happy ending and for baddies to be punished, what we are in fact longing for is the 'triumph over adversity' story – which, as Hollywood long ago discovered, is the most popular narrative of all. (It's a common myth that *EastEnders* is popular when it's depressing – it's actually more popular when characters overcome their depression and set about their everyday task of depressing others instead.)

In the late 1980s and early 1990s, when the royal family seemed to be imploding, the Windsor soap became compulsive viewing. Every day there was another tabloid headline, another lewd phone call. The royal comet appeared to be crashing to earth, culminating in the *annus horribilis*. It played out like a classic fall from grace. In soap operas, there is always a disaster that threatens the dynasty before the rebuilding begins.

In royal terms, therefore, the 'narrative' of the golden jubilee couldn't actually have happened at a better time, personifying as it does this triumph over adversity to the full. Just as in *EastEnders* we tend to use big events such as birthdays and weddings to symbolise reconciliation and forgiveness, likewise the jubilee offers a similar narrative function. The recent sad deaths of the Queen Mother and Princess Margaret actually give the jubilee a symbolic and narrative function it might otherwise have lacked. For the destruction of a dynasty followed by death followed by rebirth is an almost perfect narrative arc; the more hideous and painful the journey, the greater the sense of joy at its happy end.

Both the royal family and soap operas unite the nation and offer a sense of shared heritage. As society becomes increasingly atomised, soap operas are one of the few remaining opportunities for a national shared experience. The major events of the royal family work in similar ways. The death of Princess Diana produced an extraordinary outpouring of grief which played to the nation's collective understanding of tragic drama. It was a terrible personal and family tragedy. The fact that in fictional terms it made for perfect drama may actually go some way to explain why the nation's mourning was so powerful and extreme.

At a mythical level, nothing succeeds in exciting emotion like senseless death, particularly when it is the death of a beautiful young woman, and particularly when there are hints that she was hounded to death because of that beauty. It's interesting that whatever the reality of Diana's death (and we will never know whether her new love was eternal; whether the crash was caused by a baying pack), this is the version we all want to believe. It's fascinating too that one of the most powerful and popular stories in *EastEnders* was the death of Tiffany Mitchell, who was run down by a car outside the Queen Vic. A beautiful, flawed and misunderstood woman, she died in tragic circumstances while escaping a threatening pursuer who wanted to possess her.

### Dynasty: the royal soap

From John F. Kennedy to Prince Rainier of Monaco, the fasci-nation with dynasties is universal. Soaps directly exploit this enthralment and are almost always successful when they have a dynasty at their core. In both fact and fiction we are fasci-nated with the lives and loves, the births, marriages and funerals of the characters we have both loved and loved to hate. These big communal events act as pivotal moments in the plot. As with other soaps, it is at these moments that the royal family generates its biggest ratings.

As in life, deaths in fiction tend to focus the mind. They represent catharsis and sometimes a come-uppance. I wouldn't stress the parallels too strongly here, but it was interesting that when Princess Margaret died the reporting of her death seemed to suggest a sense of natural justice for her past excess. Her death, the story seemed to say, was a moral judgement for the way she had lived. The tension between duty and the pursuit of personal happiness is something soaps play on, and it is always present in 'The Windsors' too. It goes back to Edward VIII and Mrs Simpson, which (although once again the reality was far more complex) played out to a nation that wanted to believe in it as a classic soap opera story of love and sacrifice.

This incessant need to impose a soap narrative on royal events has of course huge dangers for the individuals concerned. Having your life played out according to dramatic convention must be extremely unsettling, and if anyone should be concerned at the moment it should be Prince Harry. The recent exposé of his experiments with cannabis suggests the classic beginnings of a Cain and Abel, 'good son/bad son' story; coincidently a story we are currently telling (with the Trueman family) on *EastEnders* too.

Whatever the reality of the royal brothers' situation, it won't be too hard – or take too many incidents – to script a possible nightmare scenario for the second-born son. It works perfectly in dramatic terms: William is the first-born so he is going to be king. Harry is left with nothing, and because that symbolic love for the future king is denied him, he becomes the dissolute one. This has little or nothing to do with the princes as real young men, but it is possible to see the beginnings of this storyline being thrust upon them. The temptation for the press to impose this line must be almost overwhelming. In the previous generation, notice how it is always Andrew who is 'linked' to supermodels and playboys in the media, while Edward is portrayed as the young buffoon. Such is the curse of narrative and our desire to see these archetypes fulfilled.

### Matriarchy: Pauline and the Queen

Perhaps the strongest parallel between TV soaps and the royal drama lies in the theme of matriarchy. There has been a strong female character at the heart of the royal story for 50 years. In British soaps, it goes back a little less far than that, but it is now hard to imagine either institution without a strong mother figure.

The reasons for matriarchal dominance in soaps are partly historical and probably stem from their origin as a means of selling detergent to women. However, this gender bias wouldn't have continued if it hadn't been successful. Like it or not, the iconic strong woman – from Ena Sharples, via Meg Richardson to Peggy Mitchell – is at the centre of every soap. The combination of power and compassion is a potent mix; the mother as head of the household, all-seeing and omnipotent, yet loving, nurturing and forgiving, seduces audiences repeatedly.

I'm not sure that soap makers even do this consciously. When we created the Slater family a couple of years ago, we did a workshop with 30 actors and assumed we would end up with a mum, dad and two kids. Instead we have a grandmother, dad, and five sisters. Furthermore, the presiding influence in the family is a dead matriarch who exerts a powerful influence on the family from beyond the grave.

However, if there is one real matriarch in *EastEnders* it is probably Pauline Fowler. I hope neither will take offence if in Pauline I see strong similarities with the Queen. Both exhibit a rich mix of suffering and duty. Pauline has tried to bring up her family as best she can, even though it hasn't always been easy. Her offspring have caused her nothing but trials and tribulations; her husband has been wayward at times and caused her several eyebrow-raising moments. But Pauline has steadfastly carried on; every morning she puts on her blue overall and goes to the laundrette. She endures, stoically and heroically, whatever life may throw at her, just as her mother did before her.

This sense of lineage is vitally important too. The fact that Pauline has been in the show since its start and was handed the role of matriarch on Lou Beale's death makes her a living embodiment of Albert Square's (read England's) history. This atavistic sensibility is a vital part of both soap and royal mythology. That sense of permanence, of moral values that survive the changing fashions of time, is central to both institutions' appeal. Whether it's true is to an extent irrelevant. The fact that so many people desire it to be true is what's important.

### A new patriarchy?

The longer we live our lives under a matriarchal structure the harder it is for us to imagine life under a king. That it is possible to imagine Charles on the throne at all, however, is a huge step forward from even a few years ago, and once again a triumph of narrative storytelling. It also, I think, tells us something new about what we value in society.

As always seems to be the case, Charles's rehabilitation arose from tragedy. Cast in the role of lone parent, he stoically dedicated himself to the role of 'good father'. The single dad is a very modern role in a traditional family setting, but it may prove significant in shaping the public's perception of King Charles.

Charles's treatment of Harry in the aftermath of the drugs stories in the papers was widely perceived as brilliant, and has obviously helped to boost him in the public's affections. That's not to say that is why he responded in that way, or that the whole unfortunate business was manipulated for PR reasons, but the episode showed the power of soap-like narratives to alter the public perceptions of the royal 'characters'.

The question now, of course, is how generations of Britons brought up under a matriarchal monarch will respond to a king. Although his sons are growing up, the role of the father may be the way in which Charles can best connect with the public. Being a good father is not something you particularly associate with kings, but our image of what makes a good man has changed a great deal over the past 50 years. The idea that a father can show emotion and the fact that Charles cried at his grandmother's funeral is now seen as a strength, whereas in the past it would probably have been seen as a sign of weakness. Did he actually cry? In narrative terms we seemed desperate to believe it true, for it makes his humanisation, his journey from devil to angel, his redemption, complete. It's a happy ending of sorts – a man who has transgressed finding his soul. Perhaps what I am describing here are the beginnings of a royal patriarchy, a new storyline we will have to start getting used to.

*John Yorke is executive producer of* EastEnders.

# Of queens and queers

The camp side of monarchy

**Andy Medhurst**

Any institution presided over by a queen is bound to be camp. I apologise for beginning with this rather obvious play on words, but if you want to try and unravel the relationship between the royal family and the British taste for camp then there are few better places to start. Playing around with the twin meanings of 'queen' (female monarch and effeminate man) may be an old joke, but we love old jokes, as our abiding affection for royalty proves only too well.

Indeed it's an older joke than most, dating back at least 400 years to the moment when steadfast, manly Elizabeth I was succeeded by the reputedly far less masculine James I, prompting the court wits of the day to comment 'The King is dead, long live the Queen'. Fast-forward four centuries to the 2001 Royal Variety Performance, and as the last line of the communally sung National Anthem melted into the theatre ceiling, there stood Julian Clary on stage, as if summoned up by that loyal chorus of 'God save the Queen'. Few jokes have such staying power, and fewer still have been adopted, even if only allegedly, by the royal family themselves. It is now part of the fabric of royal myth that the Queen Mother cracked a few funnies in this vein, once apparently curtailing a noisy party in the servants' quarters of Clarence House by asking the old queens who worked downstairs to be more considerate to the old Queen who lived upstairs. It's a good gag, and like most good gags it's also an index of a deeper cultural truth.

That pun on upper-case Queen and lower-case queen is very telling, since it is a joke about hierarchy. Those lower-case queens were also lower-class queens – not all working class, by any stretch of that always troublesome definition, but inevitably lower class when compared with the Queen Mother. By definition, nobody can be as high as those at the top. Royalty is the apex of hierarchy, the pinnacle of the status system, supplying a reference point from which those who care about such things (and in Britain, that means everybody) can measure their own standing.

## Camp goes mainstream

Decades ago, in more respectful and less sceptical times, that question of standing and those processes of measuring were matters of profound and unquestioned importance. Today, for many of us, things are very different. Royals were once virtually demigods, but now they're little more than mere celebrities, and in our fame-game culture celebrities are pawns for us to play with: snooping into their relationships, speculating about their sexual tastes, savouring their emotional crises and fashion crimes. Camp is one of the tools we use to engage with both individual celebrities and the concept of celebrity itself. Once the sole preserve of homosexual men, who used it as a bitchy guerrilla tactic for making fun of the straight world that mis-treated them, camp has in recent years gone mainstream, to the point where its cutting edge often gets lost. Even so, it remains useful for exposing hypocrisy and cutting pretence down to size, and if there is one thing we have learned about the royal family in the past couple of decades it is that they are even fonder of hypocrisy and pretence than they are of corgis. Any lingering sense of the royals as moral exemplars was shredded by seeing Diana on *Panorama*; any vestigial belief in the majesty of their majesties was flushed down the pipe by *It's a Royal Knockout*; and if we use the royal clan as a yardstick of status we do so with at least half a tongue firmly in cheek.

As their foibles and failings have become more widely known, the absurdity of uncritically venerating the royals has become obvious. It is impossible to overlook the clash between the deferential theatricality of the rituals that surround them and the knowledge we now have that they are a spectacularly dysfunctional crew, as addicted to in-fighting and back-biting as any large family. Faced with that contradiction between image and actuality, enjoying the royals as camp – as a soap opera with unusually high production values, as an all-year-round Eurovision Song Contest, or as a pantomime overstocked with hissable villains (but missing its Principal Boy since 31 August 1997) – is hard to resist.

## Camp archetypes

It is also easy to see several female members of the troupe as camp archetypes (please note that I am purposely not using the term 'gay icon', a lazy catch-all term only thought meaningful by adolescent hacks and Geri Halliwell's publicist). As long ago as the jubilee year of 1977, the academic Richard Dyer included the Queen Mother (alongside Marlene Dietrich and velvet and brocade curtains) in a list of people and artefacts he saw as inherently camp,[1] while both she and Princess Margaret have been acclaimed by the broadcaster Richard Coles as 'famous fag hags' on account of their fondness for both employing and socialising with homosexual men.[2] Evidence of this was exceedingly clear in the array of artistic chaps and endearingly effete aristocrats wheeled on to pay tributes to both women after their deaths.

Sometimes it's possible to trace elements of Hollywood's camper screen queens among the royals: Sophie Wessex seems to be pursuing Diana-hood as ruthlessly as Anne Baxter aped Bette Davis in *All About Eve*, while that news footage of Princess Margaret in her wheelchair, glaring balefully through those diva-with-a-hangover sunglasses, revealed her as a lost sister of Joan Crawford in *Whatever Happened to Baby Jane?* There are also hints of camp comedy to be found: Sarah Ferguson is a gosh-awfully galumpher straight from Joyce Grenfell's repertoire, while the Queen herself, though less immediately camp than most of her female relatives, comes more and more to resemble Stanley Baxter's drag impersonation of her with each Christmas Day broadcast.

**1** In an article published in the Canadian gay journal *The Body Politic*, and later reprinted in his collection *The Culture of Queers* (London: Routledge, 2002).

**2** Richard Coles, 'Feelin's', in Mandy Merck (ed), *After Diana: irreverent elegies* (London: Verso, 1998), p 176.

The most intriguing figure of all in this context is Princess Anne. In one of Armistead Maupin's celebrated 'Tales of the City' novels, gay San Franciscan and Anglo-kitsch *aficionado* Michael Tolliver is shopping in London for royal memorabilia. He stocks up on Diana goodies and Queen Mum trinkets but 'searched in vain for something with Princess Anne's face on it'.[3] To be a female royal and to be *not-camp* is something of an achievement, and it's an achievement that reveals plenty about our perceptions of royalty, camp and the connections between them. Anne resists the label of camp because her public image has been shrewdly crafted to make her the royal we see as most concerned with getting the job done diligently. She is direct, unfrilly, unfussily businesslike (if the royal women were Spice Girls, she would be Sensible Spice), even managing to negotiate the minefield of a broken royal marriage with considerably more aplomb than either of her similarly affected brothers. She isn't remotely masculine (though her appearance in that naval uniform at the Queen Mother's funeral made her resemble one of those dashing male impersonators who flourished in the Edwardian music hall), but she's not given to undue girlishness either.

Camp loves extravagance and ornamentation, which is why placing the Queen Mother's coffin on a pink and lavender catafalque was such a camp touch (Lavender Catafalque, it strikes me, would be a wonderful name for a drag act); but Anne has never been one for flagrant showiness. She is very much her father's daughter, and Prince Philip is to camp what Charles Hawtrey was to body-building. Philip's decidedly traditional views on gender roles are also worth bearing in mind when considering some other facets of royal lives, such as Prince Edward's ill-fated encounter with the Royal Marines and well-documented affection for the musical theatre, Prince Charles's commendably non-macho interest in New Age thinking, and even Prince William's choice of degree subject. Art History is scarcely the most overwhelmingly butch of academic disciplines, and discussions arc apparently already underway about William's possible military career after graduating, disclosing yet again the royals' quaint belief that, even

3 Armistead Maupin,
*Babycakes* (London:
Black Swan, 1984),
p.170.

after the Edward debacle, a spell in the forces will ensure the instilling of old-school masculinity.

As the incident in Maupin's novel indicates, another facet of royal camp is the role it plays in the marketing of heritage. Palaces are camp. Pomp is camp. Trooping the Colour is camp (especially when it involves those regiments most fabled in gay folklore for their after-dark availability, offering a little cavalry-shaped consolation to the Whitehall gentlemen who cruise St James's Park before going home to the wife). Yet all of these would be considerably less camp if they did not involve a living, breathing royal family. Monuments of a vanished royal past have some camp mileage (as a day trip to Versailles will prove), but they cannot compare with the fact that in Britain these people still exist, still dress up in those Barbie-goes-to-Ruritania clothes and still keep straight faces amid all those salutes and curtsies. The royals bestow palpably make-believe titles on each other (to call someone the Earl of Wessex is tantamount to calling him the Arch-Vizier of Narnia) and then carry on as if they had real meaning. The royals are as camp as they are because they give the illusion that all those rigmaroles and protocols still matter, as I am sure they do if you are so enmeshed in them that their ridiculousness isn't perceptible.

### The Queen Mummification of a nation

Around this point, however, the campness can start to curdle, since what I see as the overblown camp ceremonial of royal occasions also contributes significantly to Britain's besotted-ness with looking backwards. It seemed to me that every third caller to radio phone-ins around the time of the Queen Mother's funeral was uttering the same mantra: no other country could put on a show like this. Perhaps not, but which other country would want to? It was indeed a magnificently staged occasion, but it was not so much the funeral of an indi-vidual as the Queen-Mummification of a nation, encasing Britain in the enveloping folds of times gone by. It revealed that the mythological weight of a fantasised past still exerts an enormous emotional pull for those reluctant to address the complexities of the present, let alone think about the possibil-ities of the future.

Faced with that kind of smothering retrospection, a camp view of royalty, for all the fun it affords, can seem rather flimsy. Those discourses of deference and hierarchy are still very much alive, albeit outmoded and waning with every passing year. Their persistence suggests that a camp interpretation of the royal circus is not enough, that mocking its absurdities needs to be accompanied by a more sustained and reflective critique. Such reflections can be found elsewhere in this collection.

*Andy Medhurst teaches in the School of Cultural and Community Studies at the University of Sussex. His book* A National Joke: popular comedy and English cultural identities *will be published by Routledge later this year.*

# Part 5

## The wide world over

# Decline or fall?

The survival threat to twenty-first century monarchies

## Ken Gladdish

Kings go back a long way: to the first states, or empires, founded on conquest, of which the king was the unifying symbol and military guarantor. The alternative, explored by the Greeks and Romans, was oligarchic rule in republics. Over the last 3,000 years, in Europe at least, kings have outscored republics by a huge margin. Until 1793, only Switzerland and the United Provinces of the Netherlands lacked a king, or some equivalent.

A vast amount of Western political philosophy has understandably therefore been devoted to monarchy. It has been presented in an array of moral and historical terms, above all as an institution on which the integrity of nations and empires depended.

Four central elements of kingship stand out:

- the evolution of kings from elected war leaders to hereditary rulers
- the church's endorsement of the sacredness of monarchy
- the concept of sovereignty which promoted monarchs beyond the  feudal contract and put them above the law
- the absolute distinction of rank between royalty and its subjects.

Where monarchy survives, these elements are still discernible to some degree. The bicycling royals of Scandinavia may seem far removed from such powerful phenomena, but their status still reflects them. So do the attitudes of most of their subjects, for whom centuries of conditioning have bred an acquiescent view largely overlooking the huge assumptions on which the institution is based.

Although Western Europe provides a number of apparently stable, popular monarchies, as an institution monarchy has gone through dramatic historical decline. Most that have survived have done so by giving up on their real function – ruling. In the main they rely on the quality of their public relations strategies to secure support. How long they can continue to mask the basic contradictions between their core identity and the changing societies in which they function remains an open question.

### Recent reversals

The events which blasted a rift valley through history after 1789 reintroduced republicanism to Europe. But the French accepted the Bourbons back in 1814 and reinvested in monarchy in 1830. It was only finally buried after the ignominious rout of Napoleon III in 1870. For the rest of the nineteenth century, all the way up almost to the First World War, there were no more serious republican episodes in Europe. Even more significantly, new states sought, at whatever cost, to be monarchies. Greece, reconstituting a political identity after two millennia, recruited first a Bavarian, then a Danish prince to deliver the magic deal. Belgium also imported a German prince; and as late as 1905 the freshly liberated Norwegians voted in a referendum four to one against a republic. This was despite the need to borrow a prince from their historic overlords the Danes.

Possession of a king went with a flag, an army, a *corps diplomatique*. No new or revived polity was properly dressed or equipped without a uniformed demigod in a palace, surrounded by royal guards who both sartorially and acoustically could match the entourages of visiting rulers. Far from oblivion, monarchy had in fact been secured after 1815 by the adroit device of constitutionalism. At least in Europe. Postcolonial Latin

America, with exceptions in Brazil and Napoleon III's sad attempt to saddle Mexico with an emperor, went overwhelmingly for the North American model with a congress and a president. All they borrowed from Europe were the uniforms.

The second half of the nineteenth century saw the icono-clastic left assail all traditional institutions. But monarchies were only seriously threatened where political fluency was in jeopardy. One of the rare cases where a monarch was actually sacked, his predecessor having been murdered, was Portugal in 1910. Its Spanish neighbour had briefly tasted a republic in the 1870s, but the crown was restored and endured until 1931. There followed the Second Republic, Franco and then a remarkable restoration of the Spanish monarchy – with the same ruling family – in 1975.

## Durability and decline

That monarchy has anywhere outlived the lapse of its central function – ruling – may seem testimony to its durability. For example, in 1975 Sweden transferred all remaining royal pre-rogatives to the Speaker of the Riksdag. Yet a king the descendant of one of Napoleon's marshals – still reigns in Stockholm. If Norway had joined the European Union, half of its members would be monarchies.

In fact, the durability of the remaining few belies a major historical change over the last century. If 1789 was a watershed in European history, 1918 was even more so. New nineteenth-century states may have cast around for kings, but, with the very partial exception of Yugoslavia, none of the numerous new European states after the First World War did so. Austria, Czechoslovakia, Poland, Ireland, Finland and the Baltic states all emerged as republics. Three former massive empires, Germany, Russia, and the Ottoman, now Turkey, joined them. After the Second World War, more states – Italy, Hungary, Romania and eventually Greece – joined the republican pack. The true picture therefore is not one of monarchical survival, but of its successive dwindling. There are no kings or queens east of Sweden, and the EU contains the only surviving European monarchies, apart from Norway.

The question we might therefore ask is why Scandinavia, the

Low Countries and Britain (Spain can fairly be considered a special case) should have retained this ancient institution, when everybody else has discarded it. There appear to be two answers. The first is that for monarchies to have survived, they have obviously yielded to constitutions which have deprived them of all executive power. Where that compliance was insufficient, as in the case of the second German Reich, kings or emperors have ultimately been jettisoned.

The second is that monarchies have disappeared when the entire regime, with royalty at its masthead, has disintegrated in the face of internal or external onslaught. Kaiser William II ended up as a pensioner in Holland for both reasons: the shattering of a state where the monarch retained much power through massive military defeat.

The pathology of regime collapse is complex. The Greek monarchy survived defeat and occupation in the 1940s, but succumbed to a tacky military coup in the 1960s and was not subsequently reinstated. In Italy the collapse of Fascism brought down with it the House of Savoy. During the Second World War, Norway, Denmark and the Low Countries were occupied by Germany, but all recovered their territory intact and only in Belgium was the retention of the monarchy questioned. In Norway, the Netherlands, and to some extent the UK, monarchs became symbols of national resistance, shoring them up against radical postwar challenge.

In this context it is worth asking why up until 1918 states sought monarchs, but thereafter went exclusively for republics? Until the First World War monarchy conveyed status. The great powers, except for France, were all monarchies. Any new state was therefore bound to believe that equal terms with the other powers required royalty with all the trimmings. In the Teutonic invasions following the collapse of the Roman Empire, kings had been war leaders. The linkage between sword and sceptre had always characterised monarchy, which explains why military defeat is so often mortal for dynasties.

After 1918, there was a profound revulsion against old order militarism. New states saw themselves as part of a league of peace-promoting nations and crowned heads seemed antithetical to that project. Further, monarchy had always been at the summit of an aristocracy. But the age of aristocrats was surely over.

Even before the French Revolution, the USA, a new state which rebelled against and rejected for itself a crowned head, had prescribed equality of status (except for slaves) and pro-scribed titles of nobility. In new states like Finland and Ireland, that was the only possible position, especially where both were reacting against foreign royal rule.

Anti-militarism, social equality and, except for victorious Britain, the collapse of kingship among the great powers in 1918 suddenly reversed the quest for the status conferred by having your own monarch. There was a conferment of monarchy in the Middle East, where Britain saw advantages in installing kings in Iraq, Transjordan and Saudi Arabia, successor states to the Ottoman Empire. Within Europe, however, only Albania and Spain under Franco saw the post-1918 situation differently.

This sea change did not destroy support for monarchy where it had survived. In fact, the retention of a crowned head could be read as a measure of stability in a volatile world. Once monarchy had been reduced to a largely ceremonial role, it provided both a practical and a decorative way of supplying a head of state. Its assets were identity, a habit of deference, non-partisanship and continuity.

## Prospects for the future

Monarchical survival in the twenty-first century is at risk, but not because it is dysfunctional as a mechanism, as some claim. Rather, its indispensable ingredient – royalty – has lost not merely its mystique, but its inherent plausibility. The legiti-macy of royalty as a separate order of humanity has been under threat ever since distinctions of rank were challenged in the late eighteenth century. Since then the defence of majesty has been mounted increasingly in terms of service rather than of justified privilege. But the service provided by royalty is very difficult to separate from privilege.

We have moved from a position where the monarch was an authoritative fact, sanctioned by divine grace, to one where his or her fate rests on the effectiveness of pro-royal PR. This may seem a hopeless finale. But there is still room for a remobilisation, if not of reverence, then of popularity and affection.

If monarchy's stock has declined, the societies that still harbour it are, currently at least, drunk on celebrity. For now, royalty has the option of extending its lease by buying in glamour. The late Princess Diana in Britain was a vivid example who magnetised the public. In the Netherlands, Princess Maxima, the Argentinian wife of the Dutch heir, is another. How long such a strategy can be effective is an open question. If a new tsunami of political and social change were to inundate Europe, the remaining monarchies could be finally submerged.

*Ken Gladdish is Senior Research Fellow in Politics at the University of Reading.*

# Republican monarchy

The political necessity of the Spanish monarchy

## Shaun Riordan

The constitutional head of the Spanish state is the king. And yet Spain cannot really be called a monarchy. The current incumbent, Juan Carlos, is widely popular, and few actively want rid of him. But even fewer Spaniards would describe themselves as monarchists. Spain as a society is obsessed by gossip and the private lives of celebrities. Yet few rumours appear in the press about the Spanish royal family.

The roots of these apparent contradictions lie in Spanish history, and in particular the political history of the last 30 years. The Spanish have not had a lot of luck with their monarchs over the last 400 years. The last who could be described as 'great' was Felipe II in the sixteenth century (also, as it happens, for five years King of England). Since then, and until modern times, Spain suffered a dismal succession of in-bred Habsburgs and dissolute Bourbons. If the Spanish republic of the 1930s was hardly a success, even Franco, after the Civil War, was in no hurry to restore what was, by then, a thoroughly discredited monarchy.

The auguries for Juan Carlos did not look good either. Franco, casting around for a trustworthy successor, or at least one whom his henchmen would be able to control, lit upon the teenage son of the exiled heir to the throne. Separated from his father, he was brought up in Spain as a loyal lieutenant of the

Franco regime. His acceptance of the succession from Franco was seen as treachery by those loyal to his father. For the left-wing opposition, and even for the democratic right, Juan Carlos was seen as simply a Francoist stooge. And yet, from this inauspicious beginning, within six years of Franco's death he was seen as the symbol, and guarantor, of Spanish democracy. How did this transformation come about?

Firstly, the continuation of the monarchy became the touch-stone of the army's acceptance of the transition to democracy. The price for the legalisation of the Communist Party, for example, was the party's acceptance of the monarchist flag (albeit without Franco's eagle). The fledgeling Socialist Party followed suit. Even then, Juan Carlos was no more than tolerated by most Spaniards. Few saw him as more than a temporary fixture on the constitutional scene.

This all changed on the night of 23 February 1981. That afternoon a moustachioed Guardia Civil colonel called Tejero marched into the Spanish parliament and launched a *coup d'état* against democracy. It is difficult for many foreigners, looking at Spain today, to recall how close Tejero brought Spain to the abyss. Tanks were deployed on the streets of Valencia in support of Tejero. Other military commanders hesitated between supporting the coup or democracy. For several hours the future of Spain hung in the balance. Then, in the early hours of the morning, the King appeared on television declaring for democracy and calling on the military commanders to do the same. They did so, and the coup quickly collapsed. Its leaders, including the Spanish Chief of Staff, were arrested and put on trial, and Spain returned to the path of modernity.

The King's appearance on television that night and his role in defeating the coup have acquired almost mythical significance in Spain. With the entire Spanish political elite, including both outgoing and incoming prime ministers, held hostage in the parliament, the King was just about the only political figure at liberty. In the eyes of many Spaniards, he stood alone against the hardline elements in the army in defence of their freedom and democracy, and won. It would be a courageous commentator who questioned the King's role that night, and that person would be very unlikely to get published, in Spain at least.

## Reconciliation and unification

Subsequently the King came to play an important role in the healing of the wounds of the Franco dictatorship. If Spain consciously decided to base its transition to democracy on reconciliation, agreeing to forgive the wrongs of both sides, this was in many respects symbolised by the King. In this he was helped greatly by his personality. If few of his closest supporters would make great claims for his intellect, even fewer of his sternest critics would deny his warmth and personal charm. Not a few dyed-in-the-wool republicans have been disarmed by his self-deprecating sense of humour. He has an ability to connect with ordinary Spaniards that contrasts strongly with the dour and stuffy image of the Windsors.

The King has also played another important role in modern Spain. Spain has teetered on the brink of disintegration for the last 200 years. During the twentieth century, Basque and Catalan (and, to a lesser extent, Galician) nationalism developed a strong sense of identity different from that of the rest of Spain. Both Cataluña and the Basque Country are currently ruled by nationalist parties that claim the right to self-determination and aim, at least implicitly, for some form of separation or distancing from the Spanish state. For many from these regions, the King can symbolise a national coherence in a way that a Spanish prime minister (socialist or conservative) cannot. Juan Carlos has been careful to play this role, consciously cultivating leading nationalist politicians.

The upshot is that the success and future of the Spanish monarchy is tied closely to the figure and personality of the current king. Spaniards are not monarchists but Juan Carlists. The king has a very limited constitutional role (far smaller than that of the British monarch), and the constitution is, to all intents and purposes, republican. And yet Juan Carlos remains, for many Spaniards, almost a symbol of Spanish democracy. It is debatable to what extent his personal popularity extends to the rest of his family, or to the monarchy as an institution, and whether it can long survive him.

The personal popularity of Juan Carlos, and his symbolic role, have much to do with the respect with which the Spanish press treats the royal family. The Spanish media are certainly not shy about the private lives of celebrities. Although there is no equivalent to the British gutter press (in large part because Spain doesn't have the mass newspaper readership of Britain), there are any number of weekly magazines and television programmes (in Spain known as the pink press – *la prensa rosa*) which cheerfully pick over the private scandals of the great and not so good. The Spaniards have a voracious appetite for such revelations, and the pink press provides the staple of conversation over the tapas. Equally, Spain is no stranger to financial scandal. Felipe Gonzalez's government ended particularly mired in scandals of illegal party financing and influence peddling. Aznar's current government has so far avoided a similar reputation, but has had scandals of its own. And yet the Spanish press is extremely coy about its royal family.

### Media and the rumour mill

This is not because of any formal statute against criticism, nor because Spaniards in general are less censorious of the private lives of their political figures. Nor is it necessarily true that the Spanish royal family is whiter than white. Rumours circulate among the chattering classes that, whether justified or not, would certainly make it into the British tabloid press (if not provoke yet another *Guardian* campaign for a republic). But none of this appears in the Spanish press. At an editorial level, the press has adopted its own self-denying ordinance against overt criticism of the royal family. This is hardly ever criticised by journalists themselves, even those of an openly republican persuasion.

In part, as already suggested, this reflects the personal popularity of the current king. Yet it also goes deeper. Spain is still, at least for a foreigner, suprisingly unsure of the solidity of its democracy and constitution. Where foreigners see a modern democratic state integrated into the European Union, many Spaniards are still only too conscious of how recent all this is (Tejero's coup was, after all, only 21 years ago). Most Spanish journalists, and particularly those of the transition generation, see themselves as the guardians of Spain's democracy. They are extremely cautious of launching anything that might put that democracy in danger. While attacking elected politicians, including prime ministers, is part of the normal political game, anything that might bring into question the monarchy is seen as unacceptably risky and irresponsible. There are cans of worms which are definitely best left unopened.

**An uncertain future**

It is questionable how long this will last. The feeling is notice-ably less strong today than five years ago. The royal family is becoming almost tangibly less relevant, and visible, in Spanish life. Ironically, the centre-right government seems to feel less need to play the royal card than its socialist predecessor. The heir to the throne, Prince Felipe, has so far failed to capture the affection of the Spanish people in the manner of his father, and has little if any hope of having the same political symbolism. There is no significant pressure to abolish the monarchy, but equally little loyalty to the institution itself, as distinct from the current incumbent. It is an open question, and not at all a treasonable one, how long the monarchy will survive after Juan Carlos.

The Spanish monarchy is very different from its British equivalent. There is probably little the House of Windsor can learn from the House of Bourbon. The Spanish royal family is less visible and undertakes fewer royal duties (although those it does undertake are probably more enjoyable for the recipi-ents). It has little formal constitutional role. No one would claim it seriously enhances Spain's image abroad, or con-tributes to Spain's earnings from tourism (the 14 million Britons who visited Spain last year did not do so because of the monarchy). At the same time it costs the taxpayer significantly less than the House of Windsor. The cost of the Spanish royal family is spread among a number of different government budgets, and is therefore less public than the British civil list. But the Spanish king enjoys neither the extensive personal patrimony nor the generous government subventions of Queen Elizabeth.

The Spanish public tend to view the British monarchy with an almost voyeuristic curiosity. In part, it is classed with other British eccentricities such as the House of Lords, cricket, and warm beer. But it is also soap opera. The scandals of the House of Windsor are followed avidly in the pink press. The death of Diana provoked genuine grief in Spain, with hundreds queueing to sign condolence books in the British embassy and consulates. (Although few turned up to sign the condolence book for the Queen Mother.)

The fundamental difference between the Houses of Windsor and the Bourbons is of history. The British monarchy is the product of centuries of political evolution, with the odd civil war thrown in. It has been able to reinvent itself several times. The longer historical view of the Spanish monarchy would be of 300 years of almost unrelieved disaster and fiasco. The current Spanish monarchy is the product of very recent historical accident. Spain accepted Juan Carlos because he was politically necessary. He has continued because he was, and remains, politically necessary. The future of the monarchy in Spain will depend, in large part, on how confident the Spanish feel about the solidity of their democracy, and whether they believe the monarchy is still necessary to guarantee it. For most Spaniards there will be little emotional cost in dispensing with the monarchy once it has served its purpose.

*Shaun Riordan is an ex-diplomat and is now director of the Madrid-based consultancy companies ZEIA and New Forum. His book,* Goodbye Ambassador: towards a new diplomacy, *is being published by Polity Press later this year.*

# Postmodern monarchies

How royalty unites diversity in the Low Countries

## Wim Mellaerts

The Netherlands and Belgium have had a constitutional monarchy since 1814 and 1831 respectively – relatively late in a comparative European perspective. The history and mythology of these nations are associated with the abolition of aristo-cratic grandeur and arcane, semi-feudal power structures, so that when they became monarchies the head of state was forced to live with strong civic and republican traditions. Monarchs were never seen or portrayed as chosen by God, in part because they didn't occupy a religious position. The first king of the Netherlands, Willem I (king from 1813 to 1840), was the son of the last stadholder, the Dutch Republic's highest public servant, a post that had been held by the House of Orange for over two centuries. Belgium's first monarch, Leopold I of Saxe-Coburg (1831–1865), and his successors were all nominally approved by parliament.

For nation-states with relatively little power, dependent on realities and forces beyond their borders, it is hardly surprising that even the history of colonial rule left few marks on the idea of monarchy. Belgian and Dutch constitutional theory was rel-atively quick to model itself on British lines in restricting royal authority. Yet royal influence remained reasonably strong well into the twentieth century. Up until the Second World War, the Dutch and Belgian heads of state continued to exert considerable influence over foreign, defence and colonial policy. Nevertheless, rapid modernisation, the broadening of the electorate, and the rise of socialism made the direct interference of the monarch in politics increasingly controversial, and royal influence gradually declined.

The accession of Queen Wilhelmina (reigned 1898–1948) and King Albert I (1909–1934) opened a new era: a reinvented monarchy, more politically neutral, enjoying growing popularity and supported by a political elite that appreciated its symbolic function in a democratic, divided and secularising society. Successive monarchs and political leaders have managed to ensure continuing public respect for the institution by maintaining its position above party politics.

The most lively of all conflicts in Belgium are the complex ethnic-linguistic and regional differences between Dutch-speaking Flemings and French-speaking Walloons. Under King Baudouin (1950–1993) the monarchy continued to be seen by many Flemings as pro-francophone. Under King Albert II, the country's present monarch, and Crown Prince Filip, the monarchy has tried to distance itself from these associations. It has come to accept the devolution of power to the country's member states, without viewing it as a danger to Belgium's unity. Filip's choice of marriage partner was symbolically significant: Princess Mathilde satisfied both sides of the country's divide by coming from French-speaking Wallonia but having a Flemish name and relatives living in Flanders.

The separation of church and state may have prevailed, yet there were and still are ties between the Belgian Crown and Catholicism and between the House of Orange and the fiercely Protestant Dutch Reformed Church. The sister of Queen Beatrix, Princess Irene, caused a scandal in 1964 when she joined the Catholic Church after marrying the Spanish Prince Hugo Carlos de Bourbon – it had been customary that Dutch royals were members of the mother church. By contrast, the spouse of the heir to the throne, Prince Willem-Alexander, a Roman Catholic Argentine called Máxima Zorreguieta, has not been forced to convert to Protestantism. Their Dutch Reformed wedding service in February 2002 incorporated Roman Catholic elements in the interests of religious balance, yet this raised few eyebrows – demonstrating the success of the monarchy in freeing itself from the bonds of traditional etiquette.

## A living symbol

By placing itself above religious and national divisions, the royal family has to some extent shielded itself from controversy. But the popularity of the royals in the Low Countries is also related to the establishment's ability to convey the image of a monarch in tune with the times. This is most apparent in the Dutch case. Like her predecessors, Queen Beatrix is seen to represent the best of her country at home and abroad – undoubtedly one of the major sources of her prestige and moral authority. Through her speeches, state visits and charitable endeavours, she is seen as a living symbol of what it is that makes Dutch society special.

Since the 1990s, when questions of national identity re-entered public debate, national symbols, including the House of Orange, have been back in fashion. Yet contemporary Dutch society has also become much more fragmented, fractious and multicultural, and definitions of national identity are consequently more pluralist and diffuse. In a way, the House of Orange has re-emerged as a potent national icon because it is more flexible and open to reinvention than symbols such as national hymns or flags.

The Dutch – or at least influential constituencies such as the their political elite and media – present themselves as down to earth, competent, quietly bourgeois, and egalitarian. Queen Beatrix understands this: she exudes Dutchness. She has pulled off the trick of appearing to be just like a regular person. For instance, she knows how to demonstrate humility and simplicity (the original 'bicycling monarch'), professionalism and thrift (for instance by confining the royal dynasty to the immediate family and providing value for money), and is keen to avoid ostentation or snobbery. The Queen receives about £2.3 million a year from the state, while the total allowance (for the Queen and four other royals) comes to just over

£4 million a year. She is also extremely reserved towards the press and wary of the risks of adopting a celebrity persona – all qualities the Dutch greatly appreciate.

But perhaps more importantly, like Dutch nationalism, Dutch royalism occupies the mind of only a minority. Many feel proud of their queen, but above all, their approach to the monarchy is pragmatic, unambiguous and relaxed. The recent controversy about the father of Prince Willem-Alexander's bride is a good example: his link to the Argentinian military dictatorship of Jorge Videla was an affront to the Dutch reputation for democracy and defending human rights, but most of the population was realistic and generous about Willem-Alexander's choice.

Belgians are even greater realists, relatively impervious to grand visions or high-flown rhetoric. Most Belgians combine their national identity easily with a subnational identity (principally Flemish or Walloon) and a sense of European-ness. But more importantly, they take a highly ambivalent and sceptical attitude towards all shades of national identity and all forms of central authority. Whereas Dutch streets, shops and even some houses are periodically decked out in orange, such a degree of affection for the royal family is unheard of in Belgium. In 1999, commentators noted that the large masses expected to flock to Brussels to see the Crown Prince getting married failed to materialise. It is common to hear the expression of such sentiments as 'Belgians are no longer proud of their country', 'a national character does not exist', or, on the occasion of the recent birth of Filip and Mathilde's daughter, 'Belgium is more likely to watch the election of a European president than the coronation of a Queen'.

Very few would admit to being Belgian nationalists, and equally few would claim to be monarchists. Yet the majority, north and south of the linguistic boundaries, are sympathetic towards the House of Saxe-Coburg. Although Belgians are rarely preoccupied with the royals and consider them no better than ordinary folk, they are also secretly fond of their royalty. The relationship of the great majority to the monarchy is thus paradoxical: public indifference, below which lies a mixture of mockery, distrust and pride (usually on display only at special occasions).

It is precisely such negative affirmations that fill the void of public lack of interest, and which provide Belgians with an understated sense of admiration for their royals. This is monarchism, albeit of a rather strange variety. Albert and Filip know how to play on these sentiments: even more aware of their limits than their Dutch counterparts, they are at ease with a multinational Belgium and a European federation. They hesitate to set the royal family up as an example to others, and maintain a distinctly low profile. The media and public response to the Delphine affair (involving an alleged illegitimate daughter of King Albert) is illustrative of the insouciance and relaxed expectations of royalty among Belgians. The Belgian media largely ignored the problems in the King's marriage – it was generally agreed that the private life of members of the royal family should remain private.

## A democratic paradox?

It perhaps seems strange that, despite the importance the inhabitants of the Low Countries attach to the principles of democracy, meritocracy and rationality, they still support the idea of a hereditary head of state. Sections of the media, the political world and academia – especially in the Flemish-speaking part of Belgium – may mutter about republicanism, but the public at large scarcely question the existence of a hereditary monarchy or the exercise of royal power. Currently the monarchy is in rude health. In the Netherlands it has become ever more entrenched in recent years, and even in Belgium, republicanism is restricted to a few Flemish nationalists and extreme-left critics. This seems doubly strange if one considers that the Dutch and Belgian monarchs are not strictly ceremonial heads of state. Although they can be virtually ignored by the government from a political point of view, they still hold residual prerogatives and exercise influence behind the scenes. The monarch is formally part of the executive branch of government, nominally appoints ministers, signs all legislation – although it is only valid if countersigned by a minister – and has the nominal right to dissolve parliament.

Most significant is their advisory role in cabinet formation. Formally speaking, the monarch takes the initiative in forming governments when he or she appoints an *informateur* or *formateur*, after taking soundings from representatives of the political parties and parliament. By suggesting certain coalitions (a necessity in Dutch and Belgian politics), the monarch has considerable discretionary power to keep the process going. With elections by proportional representation and the lengthy negotiations that follow, the head of state could easily get involved in politics full-time. The impact of royal advice or requests is difficult to estimate. In theory and practice, though, the head of state cannot act against the advice of ministers.

## Monarchy as stability

Similarly, it is not unheard of for the monarch to assume a partisan position, albeit with government approval. This happened in 1996 when King Albert filled the vacuum left by the government and law courts, lambasting them for failing to protect the country's children in the wake of the Dutroux scandal and calling for a review of the judicial system. Albert's intervention in the governmental crisis was the defining moment in his reign so far, and it seems that the political establishment and public opinion are united in their appreciation of the monarch as a stabilising factor. They appear to agree that in a country with a lot of potential internal conflicts, and where cabinet formation is often difficult, it is important that the monarch, as a figure above party politics, has a role to play in bringing together parties, ideological groups or linguistic communities. Crucial to understanding this is that the fact that Belgium and the Netherlands were and still are countries obsessed with securing domestic stability and minimising internal differences.

In Belgium, King Baudouin was seen to play a marked role in this respect throughout much of the late 1970s and 1980s, years of political turmoil and instability that stemmed from intercommunal tensions and a precarious economy. Some political groups such as D66, a Dutch progressive-liberal party, have suggested that the monarch has no right to intervene – that the duties of the head of state should be restricted to purely ceremonial ones – but no other politicians have seen fit to challenge the status quo.

One can argue that the respect for the monarchy in the Low Countries is maintained by the way in which their heads of state, at critical junctures, have carefully managed to play a temporising and refereeing role. This respect has been enhanced by the manner in which their political leaders have (when it suited them) cultivated the image of the monarch as a reliable king-arbitrator (*vide* Belgium) or a stable supervisory power above the political parties (*vide* the Netherlands).

The vestigial official powers will probably be scaled back further when the next generation of monarchs takes over, yet they are unlikely to disappear, at least in the short term. The constitutional crisis that followed Baudouin's refusal in 1990 to sign a law legalising abortion, and questions about the competence of Filip, have pushed this debate up the agenda in Belgium.[1] Similarly, in 1996, much to the public's surprise, Beatrix strongly opposed the legalisation of gay weddings, which sparked some debate in the Netherlands.

But there are also forces slowing down the process. As citizens in both countries have increasingly come to see themselves as able to make better decisions for themselves than the political parties do (and, in the Belgian case, as politicians have lost credibility in the atmosphere of scandal of recent years), one might speculate that the idea of monarchy *à la belgo-hollandaise* will once more be seen as politically useful in helping to bridge the growing gulf between voters and politicians, and that popular support for the monarchy's political powers will become more secure.

1 King Baudouin withheld the Royal Assent, allowing his Catholic views to prevail over his constitutional role. He then abdicated for a few days (via a constitutional loophole which allowed the government to ratify the law), until parliament voted him back in.

*Wim Mellaerts is Lecturer in Dutch at University College London.*

# On their bikes

Will Belgium create a democratic monarchy?

**Reinout Goddyn**

The monarchies of Belgium and Great Britain both rest on 'parliamentary democracy with constitutional monarchy'. But public appreciations of the royal houses are very different. Could it be that the difference lies in the way the monarchs interpret their constitutional position to fit the needs of contemporary society?

Belgium's commercial television channel VTM, together with the weekly magazine *Story*, recently asked their viewers and readers to rank well-known royal personages on a series of issues. According to this poll, Queen Elizabeth is the least elegant of all European queens. The British royal couple has the least radiance. The love affair between Charles and Camilla scores lowest in the list of 'most beautiful royal romances'. And Prince Charles is the least charismatic of all European crown princes. To close the list, nine people in ten defined Queen Elizabeth II as the most unsuitable grandmother of all European kings and queens.

Yet when asked 'Who is the most unforgettable royal figure of the twentieth century?' more than half of the contributors named Diana, Princess of Wales. She scores better than the Belgians' 'own' King Baudouin, who died in 1993, Princess Grace of Monaco, or Queen Astrid of Belgium – whose death provoked a remarkably similar response to that of Princess Diana – both were tremendously popular women.

Of those who replied, 73 per cent said that Prince William was the 'cutest' of all the European princes and princesses. The poll was organised two months after the documentary on Prince William's gap year activities in Chile was broadcast on Belgian television.

These results show only the superficial opinion of a small part of the population. And the grades given to individual personal characteristics have little influence on the general public's appreciation of the monarchy as an institution. When contributors were asked how Elizabeth performs as head of state, she scores better than, say, Prince Hans-Adam of Liechtenstein or King Mohammed VI of Morocco.

In 1815, the British regent was so deeply hated by the people that he didn't dare appear in public. Yet his daughter, Charlotte, Princess of Wales, was tremendously loved, and the monarchy as an institution remained popular.

During the Second World War, the Belgian government fled to Britain, while King Leopold III remained in the country. The government declared that the King was 'not able to exert his powers'. The situation could have been normalised after the war. But, by then, the differences between government and King had grown so deep that ministers appointed his brother Charles as regent. The institution remained, the person was changed. Only five years later a referendum returned the constitutional powers to King Leopold.

Last year's survey found that support for the Belgian monarchy as a form of government was strong and stable, and that approval of King Albert and Queen Paola was high, in marked contrast to the personal ratings of the British monarch.

Why are the two royal houses judged so differently? They are based on roughly the same principles of government. The only differences lie in personal style, and in the way in which the members of the royal house interpret their prerogatives.

**Common roots**

When the founding fathers of Belgium in 1830 discussed a suitable form of government, they almost unanimously agreed on a hereditary monarchy. But while the constitutional assembly wanted a monarchy from which they could draw stability, continuity and order, they wanted to restrict the king's personal power. The political position of the monarch is summed up in this article of the constitution: 'No decision of the king is valid unless it is also signed by a minister, who is responsible for that decision.'

When Prince Leopold I of Saxe-Coburg became Belgium's first king, he was already the 41-year-old widower of Charlotte, Princess of Wales. He had lived in the UK for 16 years, and brought his ideas about the British monarchy with him.

The only obvious difference from the British constitutional role is that the head of state in Belgium cannot be the head of a church. The system allows for an enormous margin of personal interpretation. Theoretically, a king can rule authoritatively, making all decisions by himself, and summoning his ministers to co-sign the decisions. Or he can sit back and relax, have the government do all the work and just put his signature on any papers that are put on his desk.

The lesson of history, however, is that whenever a king has tried to assert his authority, it has been contained by law. Over time, many of the royal prerogatives have been eroded.

### Clashes with the constitution

The first Belgian king, Leopold I, called the system of parliamentary constitutional monarchy 'monstrous' and 'absurd' in letters to his beloved niece, Queen Victoria, in Britain. Leopold was born under the *ancien régime* of Saxe-Coburg-Saalfeld. By the time he was 21, his contact with several types of government had led him to develop political ideas that inspired him to instigate a form of parliament in the little Duchy of Coburg. In Britain between 1820 and 1831, he visited industrial towns in Scotland and Wales, predicted the rise of what would later be called socialism, and pleaded for a (limited) shift of power from princely families towards citizen-politicians. Yet, during his reign in Belgium, he almost constantly clashed with the limits of his constitutional freedom of movement.

King Albert also enjoyed broad constitutional liberty during and after the First World War. In that period he saw the chance to press through personally some radical change for universal suffrage. He furthered the advance of socialism by declaring the freedom of unions and personally installing socialist ministers in his cabinet against the will of powerful capitalists, allowing for a controlled development of leftist forces rather than a violent struggle with a potentially dangerous outcome – this was a year before the revolution in Russia. Even so, the King later complained about the limits of his constitutional position, describing his role as a 'misplaced joke'.

In 1950, a narrowly reinstated Leopold III found it impossible to continue in the face of riots and deep differences of opinion between king and government. When the King found not a single minister to back his decisions, he had no other choice than to resign, in favour of his eldest son, Baudouin.

Baudouin himself clashed with parliament over a law legalising abortion. Despite its approval by the rest of the constitutional apparatus, he refused to give the law Royal Assent because of his Catholic faith. Many found this an insult to democracy. Others praised the 'courage' of the monarch. Well-informed court correspondents know that many influential people, including the chief of the royal cabinet Jacques van Yperseele de Strihou, tried to persuade the King to sign. Yet the King refused.

A juridical solution was found: the government declared that the King was temporarily unable to exert his powers. In such a case, the ministers, united in council, can legally exert the power of head of state by themselves. They signed the abortion law and 24 hours later restored the King's powers. After this incident, the government immediately started working on a new variation of the constitution, in which Royal Assent cannot be subject to personal meddling by the monarch.

With every conflict, the power of the monarch has diminished. Governing is done by politicians. The king can only act in complete accordance with the political reality in the society.

### Working creatively with the constitution

If the constitution is often felt by monarchs to be a suffocating bodice, European monarchies have found many creative variations in interpreting their constitutional roles.

In the Netherlands, for example, while Queen Beatrix is formally a member of the cabinet, it is her personal authority that gives her influence. In the Scandinavian countries, most ties between the royal house and the political world were severed years ago. On a recent list of the most powerful people in her land, Denmark's Queen Margrethe ranks only 143.

But diminishing constitutional power appears to create greater freedom to act. In Romania, a country whose constitutional monarchy was abolished under communism, former King Michael I has rediscovered a role after a long period in exile. Members of the former royal family are now ordinary citizens with normal passports, but the former king and his family still carry their royal titles. King Michael has recently been given official assignments, including presiding at state banquets and coordinating reconnaissance talks with Nato. As a result he gets a pension as a former head of state, and some of his former palaces have been given back. This non-constitutional royal position allows Princess Margarita, daughter of Romania's last king, to lead a highly effective non-governmental aid fund.

Another interesting example of how the Belgian royal family uses its privileged position to serve the population is the King Baudouin Foundation. Established in 1976, on the 25th anniversary of his accession to the throne, the foundation

> *tackles social problems and challenges by stimulating solidarity and generosity, and by acting as a catalyst for sustainable change. It serves as a forum by bringing together experts and citizens, stimulating long-term thinking and increasing public awareness . . . In practical terms this means that the foundation develops initiatives in the areas of poverty and social exclusion, labour and employment, sustainable development, justice and local government, and the development of the civil society.*

While the King Baudouin Foundation is legally an independent society, its direct link with the royal house is obvious. However, legally, nobody can point a finger at the king for taking a personal action or initiative, or for expressing an opinion. Not even when the King Baudouin Foundation tackles politically highly sensitive subjects, as was the case when it awarded its prestigious development prize to the Human Rights Commission of Pakistan (1998) or the Landless Peasants' Movement of Brazil (1996).

## Reasons for preservation

If the political power of the head of state has been eroded, why then should the monarch be kept as part of the state? Stability, symbolism, inward investment and tourism are all familiar answers.

For many Belgians the king also fulfils an abstract role as a sort of glue helping to unify the French-, Flemish- and German-speaking communities into one nation.

Just five years ago, a political crisis provided another reason: the monarchy as lightning-rod. Britain was still recovering from the shock of Fred and Mary West, when Belgium, too, had its own series of child murders. More by chance than by the work of the police, recidivist Marc Dutroux was arrested after having kidnapped six children and killed four. Judge Jean-Marc Connerotte, who had saved two teenage girls from the clutches of Dutroux, was taken off the investigation because he had accepted a plate of spaghetti at a party for these two girls. His superiors judged that by doing so, he had compromised his neutrality. Belgium was shocked, not just because of the crimes, but also by the apparent failing of the political and judicial systems. Public anger resulted in the largest demonstration ever held in the capital. Some politicians feared a collapse of law and order. Politicians and royal advisers suggested a round-table conference in the royal palace, putting the parents of victims, politicians, police and magistrates in one forum. The King publicly blamed the magistrates and police for not having done what was expected of them. These actions helped to defuse the situation.

Five years after the Dutroux affaire, nothing has really changed. Sociologist Koen Pelleriaux of the University of Brussels thinks the King missed a chance. He could have worked as a catalyst towards change if he had given an example by putting aside the rules of protocol and going to the funeral of the murdered children. '*That* would have had an effect on the archaic, arrogant judiciary caste!' says Pelleriaux.

A democratic royal house can also act as a buffer against extreme right-wing politics. Kings, queens, princes and princesses can appeal to voters looking for strong, authoritative leadership. In the current environment, such an effect may be important for mainstream democracy.

### The royals and the travelling people

Will the princes and princesses of today, kings and queens of tomorrow, retain a position where they can signify something for society?

Royal players should look back on great royal personalities in the last century. Those royal figures with great charisma and popularity were the ones who were able to use their constitutional position to accomplish things for the benefit of the nation. Some individual kings and queens stand out from the rest. King Albert I of Belgium made a difference when he used his charismatic leadership to force the granting of the right to vote and to invite socialism into government against the will of the other parties. Queen Elizabeth, the Queen Mother, achieved major accomplishments during the Second World War. Princess Diana obtained huge public goodwill in the struggle against landmines and AIDS.

It is disquieting to see how little contemporary royal figures care about popularity. Some are afraid of it, some plainly hate the effect it has on their privacy. Of course, most royal personages are aware of the pitfalls of being famous. And, of course, long-term goals are more important than the small gains of superficial, short-lived popularity. But the princes and princesses who will be heads of state tomorrow will have to appeal to a greater part of society if they want monarchy to survive and prosper.

In 2002 it is easy to see how a royal house can stay in touch with its time and its people. The 'Burgundy' style of motorcyclist-king Albert is very different from the stiff 'out of this world' appearance of Queen Elizabeth. Albert appears to be a man with both feet on the ground. He loves a joke, loves contacts with people, and his calm and charismatic behaviour influences people around him. When Albert and Elizabeth met in Ypres to commemorate the end of the First World War, he greeted her with a kiss on the cheek. The Queen would never do such a thing.

I'd love to see the Queen queue in a supermarket and pay for everyday necessities. I'd love to see Prince Charles spend three days in a caravan among travelling people.

Monarchy as an institution has to change. Princes and princesses must realise that their public appearance is a part of their job. Work with popularity. Use it. Be conscious of its presence, its power, its pitfalls, but don't deny it, and don't destroy it.

*Reinout Goddyn is a photographer, writer and television journalist specialising in royal matters. His children's book* Living as a king *explains the reality of monarchy to children at an age when they realise that kings and princesses are more than just fairy-tale characters.*

# A lightly locked door

Australia and the monarchy

**Matt Peacock**

*'I did but see her passing by*
*And yet I love her till I die'*

This declaration by Australian Prime Minister Sir Robert
Menzies during the Queen's visit in 1963 drew a collective
national groan of embarrassment. Even the Queen herself, it
was reported, thought it a little over the top. Menzies was the
man who described himself as 'British to the bootstraps', the
man who had wanted to call the newly minted Australian
dollar a 'Royal'. Die-hard royalists here long ceased to be a
majority, and even as a schoolboy I thought this a bad idea.
Australia's efforts to dislodge royal power seem to arise once in
a generation. And while Australians have recently reaffirmed
the Queen as head of state, their support for the monarchy
remains shallow.

It was my generation who voted Menzies out of his two
decades of power. In 1972, Labor's Gough Whitlam swept away
a swathe of colonial baggage, along with the draft and the
involvement of Australian troops in the Vietnam War. Out
went the appeal to the Privy Council in England; in came the
Order of Australia to replace royal knighthoods. No longer did
we want God to save our Queen, but Australia Fair to Advance
in our national anthem. Sentimental affection for the Queen

remained among the Second World War generation, and some women's magazines continued to be obsessed with royalty. But for the young she was seen as an almost complete irrelevance in the political process.

That was until calamity hit the inexperienced reformist government. Money supply was blocked by a hostile upper chamber, the Senate. Whitlam was preparing to respond when he was suddenly sacked by the man he had appointed as the Queen's representative, Governor General Sir John Kerr. Sir John had exercised his 'reserve powers' – the same powers, I had learned, as a student of constitutional law, that by convention would never be used. Kerr not only used them, he went on to appoint the Opposition as Government until an election could be held.

In politics, timing is everything. The unexpected and unprecedented nature of Kerr's action placed the government in a dire situation. Usually the only real advantage an unpopular government might have is to choose the timing of an election. In this case even that had been taken from it. Politically, all hell broke loose. Unions urged a national strike. The president of the Australian Council of Trade Unions, Bob Hawke, urged them to cool it. Labor, of course, lost the subsequent election. Many Australians still regard Kerr's action as a constitutional coup. To others, it was a shadowy plot masterminded by the CIA and other security services to which Sir John had an attachment. For yet others, it was comforting confirmation of the safeguards in a system which will prevail when governments get out of control.

### Symbolic and ceremonial?

There was, however, a common thread that ran through most people's experience. Suddenly, those interested in politics gained a healthy respect for the fine print of the constitution. No more would people blithely assume that the monarch and her representative in Australia were purely symbolic figures with no real power. The Governor General had shown himself able and willing to sack a popularly elected government. It was a lesson burnt into the brains of a generation.

One of that generation was Malcolm Turnbull, then a talented debater with political ambition. Thirteen years later, he took on the defence case as the barrister for former British MI5 agent Peter Wright, who had published his *Spycatcher* memoirs. The British government's effort to silence Peter Wright created a courtroom spectacle that captured the Australian imagination. Turnbull brilliantly exploited the arrogance of the colonial masters in Whitehall, summoning and then exposing its mandarins, one of whom admitted to having been 'economical with the truth'. He became a popular champion in Australia, someone who had irreverently and successfully defied the same colonial crown authority which had previously sacked an Australian government.

Throughout this period, the monarchy in Australia was tolerated. But it became a lot less popular, particularly among those who, from the 1975 sacking onwards, had continued to respond to Gough Whitlam's urging to 'maintain your rage'. People watched the sorry saga of Charles and Camilla, and then, like Britons, wept at Diana's death. But there was no seriousness attached to their affection for the royals. It was largely media-driven. To the postwar generation, the royal family is the rough equivalent of the Simpsons, with a touch of *Dynasty*: a famous, dysfunctional family to whom they can relate, but only at a comfortable distance. That is not to say most Australians dislike the Queen. But when they think of her at all, it is as a familiar figure with whom they feel a degree of sympathy.

**Exceptional circumstances**

Indigenous Australians are an exception. By Aboriginal people the name of the Queen is invoked almost as often as that of Captain Cook, and historically the Queen has been the representative of the invaders. Recently a conservative New South Wales education minister, in a pathetic effort to whip up chauvinism, decreed that schoolchildren should salute the flag each morning. It is the Union Jack in the flag most Aboriginal Australians see, not the stars of the Southern Cross. Hence my daughter, as one of two tiny six-year-old Koori girls, was defiant as they were marched up to the headmistress. 'It's not our flag,' they told her.

The recent referendum for a republic prompted a rethink among many Aboriginal people. A number of Aboriginal politicians decided that dealing with HRH might in fact be preferable to dealing with Canberra. To sever the colonial link might mean the coming of age of the colonial descendants.

When Australia was claimed in the name of the Queen, the Letters Patent contained instructions to negotiate with the inhabitants. These instructions were conveniently ignored when the murderous settlers decided the land was empty. They thus enshrined in Australian land law the notion of *terra nullius* – 'empty land'. This legal concept that the continent was uninhabited at the time of colonial settlement persisted until the Australian High Court overturned it two centuries later. In a case brought by a Torres Strait Islander (with a Spanish forebear) named Eddie Mabo, the High Court ruled that Australia had been populated at the time of colonisation, and a residual native title to land still persisted. This has opened the way for Aboriginal native title claims to unalienated land, which in most cases is crown land. Aboriginal people continue today to pore over documents like the Magna Carta in an effort to cut out the middleman and deal direct with the British Crown.

This curious relationship between indigenous Australians and the British monarch was highlighted during the recent republic referendum, when the immediate past Governor General introduced a number of Aboriginal politicians to the Queen. In the end, a significant number urged a No vote, though in any case the total number of Aboriginal voters is miniscule.

### Long to reign over us?
The referendum debate was ignited by Labor Prime Minister Paul Keating, and stopped by John Howard, the current Liberal incumbent. The British tabloids dubbed Keating the 'Lizard of Oz' when he dared to put his arm around the Queen during a visit to London. Keating envisioned an Australia in Asia, and he wanted to weaken Australia's historical ties with Britain. Although a working-class lad from Bankstown, he had joined the new aristocracy, acquiring French antique clocks, terrace houses and an image of arrogance.

The Australian Republican Movement, formed in the early 1990s, was mainly a collection of liberal, middle-class activists well versed in the details of the Whitlam sacking and other intellectual justifications to sever ties with the Crown. Malcolm Turnbull became its leader. They had the passion of nationalists but the style of aristocrats. Like the Prime Minister, the movement gained a reputation as an elite, chardonnay-sipping society, removed from the working-class roots that had traditionally driven the Australian left.

Keating led a push to create a republic in time for the new millennium. Just like the Millennium Dome, this deadline became its kiss of death. Keating lost power; the monarchist Howard took office. He had promised Australians a refer-endum and he was true to his word. But he set the timetable, the rules and, crucially, the words to be put to the voters. The result should be no real consolation for monarchists. A majority of Australians are republicans. The problem was that they could not agree on an appropriate model. The Yes vote split, exactly as Howard predicted.

The essence of the disagreement among the republicans was how a new president should be elected. Politicians, knowing only too well how untrustworthy politicians are, feared direct election by the people. A politician would win, they warned, with the electoral mandate and reserve powers to challenge Parliament. The Australian electorate shares this distrust of politicians. It was no surprise they voted down the proposed model that suggested the new president be chosen by MPs. It was not a vote for the monarchy. It was the rejection of an unpopular model for a republic, containing within it a vote against the city elite.

That was not how it was seen at the Palace. On hearing the news, the late Queen Mother was reported to be delighted. Lord St John of Fawsley, a close friend, revealed recently that she did not conceal her delight. 'She was very, very pleased . . . and took out her glass, her favourite drink was gin and Dubonnet. When she liked something, she lifted the glass up in the air . . . and said "Good on them! Up with the Aussies!"'

### A lightly locked door

If Australians distrust their politicians, they are even more prepared to distrust foreigners. Under different circumstances, it is feasible that the same farmers who voted to keep the

Queen would vigorously campaign for her removal, if for example Prince Philip were to campaign for the revival of British beef and sheep markets to the disadvantage of Australian ones. Australian servicemen, urged to die 'For King and Country', have long wondered whose country was being talked about. And there is a high degree of cynicism among those told by the British Ministry of Defence that its nuclear tests conducted in the 1950s in Australia were to test the effects on their uniforms, not on them.

One of the ironic fallouts of the recent republican debate in Australia is that there now appears to be a much greater interest in matters royal. For a correspondent reporting from London, there is as much demand for even trivial royal stories in Australia as in the equivalent British media. As a cadet journalist I was taught that for high-rating stories, you could not beat a yarn about animal cruelty or the royal family. We seem to have reverted, although these days the stories are seen through the prism of a more active republican debate

'It's the media, stupid,' should be the Carville-like exhortation by their spinners to the royal family. So long as the current rehabilitation of the royal image continues, as Prince Charles edges Camilla closer to the throne, and as the theme-park British ceremonies continue unsullied by scandals, then the royal position in Australia will probably stay unchallenged. There is no overwhelming support for the Crown, but there is a degree of tolerant affection. The brittleness of the institution, however, can be seen in the recent controversy surrounding the current Governor General. During the Queen's most recent visit to Australia, the Governor General became enveloped in accusations that, in his previous job as a bishop, he had handled inappropriately issues of sexual abuse. Such incidents act as a boost to republican sentiment, but it will require a greater shock to galvanise republican forces into unity. The Australian monarchy remains, as Donald Horne observed nearly 40 years ago, a 'lightly locked door'.[1]

1 D Horne, *The Lucky Country* (Victoria: Penguin, 1964).

*Matt Peacock is Europe Correspondent for the Australian Broadcasting Corporation. He writes in a personal capacity.*

# Private ritual, public support

How the Japanese monarchy prepared itself
for the twenty-first century

**John Breen**

The pivotal moment in the last century of the Japanese
monarchy was, without doubt, the promulgation of the new
Japanese constitution in 1947. The constitution was the
handywork of Japan's American occupiers, and it wrought a
fundamental transformation on the emperor, the imperial
family and their relationship to power. Any discussion of
Japan's monarchy in the twenty-first century might usefully
begin by pointing up key differences between the provisions of
the new constitution, which remains in force to this day, and
those of the so-called Meiji Constitution of 1890 which it
replaced.

Meiji means 'enlightened rule', and was the name given to
the era 1868–1912. The Meiji Constitution accorded to the
Japanese emperor distinctly sacred qualities. Article 1 held
that the empire of Japan would be reigned over and ruled 'by a
line of Emperors unbroken for ages eternal'. The authority for
this assertion derived from state myths first composed in the
eighth century as a way of distinguishing Japan's sovereigns
from those of China. These myths 'proved' Japanese Emperors
were superior to those of China and elsewhere, since they

alone were descended directly from the Goddess of the Sun, Amaterasu. Article 3 of the constitution defined the incumbent of the throne as both 'sacred and inviolable'. Little wonder that the Meiji emperor and his successors came to be the focus of a quasi-religious cult. The Meiji Constitution also placed the sacred emperors at the hub of the political realm. The emperor was 'head of empire and the locus of state sovereignty'; he was commander-in-chief of the armed forces; and government ministers were defined in terms of their responsibility to him as 'imperial advisers'.

The American-penned constitution of 1947 severed the emperor's links with politics and the military and omitted all reference to his sacred qualities. Article 1 recast him as follows: 'The Emperor shall be the symbol of the state and of the unity of the people.' It continued: '[The Emperor derives] his position from the will of the people with whom resides sovereign power.' The metamorphosis worked by the constitution on the wartime emperor Hirohito was presaged by a remarkable statement he issued in New Year 1946. With the Allied Powers now dismantling the wartime state and its ideological apparatus, Hirohito declared that the bonds between emperor and people were founded 'not on myth and legend', but rather on mutual trust, affection and respect. He pointed up the fallacy of 'claiming the emperor to be a living deity' and of assuming as a consequence that the Japanese were the supreme race, destined to rule the world.

This statement and the constitution that followed quickly redefined Hirohito as a constitutional monarch. He became the symbol of Japan's new democracy; his functions were now purely ceremonial and subject to cabinet approval. Hirohito quickly embarked on a tour of Japan designed to close the previously unbridgeable gap between sovereign and people.

## Privatised ritual

What, then, are the links between the imperial institution of wartime Japan and that presided over by Akihito, the present emperor? Above all, the continuities are manifest in the rituals Akihito performs in the annual imperial cycle. There are nine 'major rites' that structure the course of the year, all of which are performed by the emperor as celebrant. These and other lesser rites all celebrate the emperor's descent in an unbroken line, generation upon generation, from Amaterasu, the Sun Goddess. In other words, Akihito recreates by his ritual actions today the mythical truth that his father denied in that famous statement of 1946. What differs of course is that the rituals Akihito performs are no longer state events, they are the strictly private affair of the imperial court. They are therefore quite constitutional.

Even as I put the finishing touches to this essay (3 April 2002), Akihito is presenting offerings to the spirit of Emperor Jinmu before the palace shrines. He is even now dispatching emissaries laden with offerings to Jinmu's mausoleum in Unebiyama, outside the city of Nara. Other major rites celebrated by Akihito in 2002 include the anniversary of Akihito's father, Hirohito, in January and the great ancestral rites of spring and autumn. Two rites especially proclaim the Emperor's intimacy with the Sun Goddess: the Kanname rite of October and the Niiname of November. In the former, Akihito will offer fruits to Amaterasu in the palace and then turn south west where, some 500 miles away, stands the Grand Shrine of Ise, also dedicated to the Sun Goddess. In the latter Niiname rite, Akihito will offer to the Sun Goddess the fruits of the rice seedlings he himself planted earlier this year. He will pray for the peace of the realm and the abundance of the rice crop, and then he will partake of the rice himself. Through the rice he consumes in the Niiname rite, the Emperor will be imbued with the Sun Goddess's invigorating spirit. He and the Sun Goddess become one.

Outwardly then the new constitution proclaims the constitutional nature of the Japanese monarchy. Indeed, Akihito in his first public address as emperor in 1989 swore to protect the constitution and carry out his responsibilities 'in line with the constitution'. His personal commitment to constitutional monarchy is not in doubt, and he presides over a range of other, purely secular rites, such as the investiture of prime ministers, receiving foreign diplomats, and awarding various orders of merit. Yet inwardly, he continues to celebrate his unique relationship with the Goddess of the Sun.

How does the imperial institution engage with the Japanese public of the twenty-first century? What does the monarchy mean to today's Japanese? A first point is that several of the imperial rites cited above double as national holidays. The Niiname rite is marked as Labour Day; the spring and autumn ancestral rites are national holidays, as are the present and last emperors' birthdays. The day of 11 February commemorates the founding of Japan by Emperor Jinmu, and is known as National Foundation Day. There is, in other words, a distinctly imperial character, though a largely covert one, to the cycle of national holidays. The efforts of right-wing lobbyists to resurrect the national holidays of wartime Japan with their much more overtly imperial character have so far achieved the one success of National Foundation Day, which was reinstituted in 1967.

## Public support

Emperor Akihito seems to enjoy genuine popularity. Surveys consistently suggest that some 70 per cent of the public support the imperial institution under his leadership. This owes much to his common touch. He met his commoner wife, the charismatic Catholic-educated Michiko, on a tennis court. Emperor and Empress make a point of getting out and about, and last year they made some 50 sorties for one purpose or another to different prefectures and cities the length and breadth of Japan. Hospitals and old people's homes as well as major sporting and cultural events are favourite stops. Akihito and his wife seem to inspire genuine affection in the Japanese they meet. He is certainly far more genial and relaxed than his father ever was.

Tens of thousands of flag-waving Japanese regularly turn up outside the balcony of the Tokyo palace at New Year and on the Emperor's birthday. In late 2001, there was a striking display of popular enthusiasm for the imperial institution when Masako, the multilingual commoner wife of Crown Prince Naruhito, gave birth to a baby girl. The national news showed crowds of people fighting to get hold of free special supplements of the left-wing broadsheet *Asahi*, issued to celebrate the imperial birth.

The prefecture Akihito has visited most in his travels is Okinawa, where for many the imperial institution still symbolises the evils of the Japanese military. He last visited in 1995 as part of a commemorative tour that also took him to Hiroshima and Nagasaki. His obviously sincere sorrow for the loss of so many thousands of Japanese and American lives won him previously unimaginable respect from many Okinawans.

**From emperor to empress?**

There is every indication that the Japanese monarchy will continue to have a role at home and abroad well into the twenty-first century. But it will first need to overcome a major crisis it is facing, relating to the fact that Masako gave birth to a girl. The new parents expressed great joy, but for the nation as a whole this was tinged with a sense of disappointment that the girl was not a boy. A supplement to the constitution stipulates in its first article that the heir to the throne must be male. Yet when Naruhito accedes to the throne on Akihito's death, there will be no male heir. No doubt Naruhito and Masako will keep trying to produce a male offspring, but time is running out.

The Japanese public is in little doubt what it thinks about the matter. When asked in a recent survey by the broadsheet *Asahi*, some 80 per cent of respondents said they would support the idea of a female acceding to the throne. Support has steadily increased over the past few decades. In the 1970s, only 30 per cent approved; in the 1990s, the figure rose to 50 per cent. The figures reflect an awareness of the practical problems, but they also reinforce other surveys which suggest there is no desire to change the constitutional, symbolic nature of the imperial institution. If the incumbent of the throne is a symbol and without political power, why can't a woman perform the task as well as a man? History would support this development, as prior to the promulgation of the prewar constitution several empresses did reign. Japan's Prime Minister, Koizumi Junichiro, has made clear he can see no objections, in principle, to resurrecting the practice. Change happens slowly in Japan. But a revision to the law to allow a woman to succeed to the throne can only enhance the popularity of the imperial institution.

*Dr John Breen is a Senior Lecturer in Japanese language and history at the School of Oriental and African Studies, London.*

# Death threat

Can Nepal's monarchy survive the massacre?

## Kanak Mani Dixit

The royal palace massacre which took the lives of King Birendra and his entire family on the night of 1 June 2001 was one more catastrophe in a harrowing series dating from 1990, when absolute monarchy was wrested from King Birendra. Even then, as the country became a parliamentary democracy and constitutional monarchy, the euphoria of the moment was tempered by an appreciation of how difficult the task ahead would be.

A polity that had been asleep for nearly three decades under the Panchayat system of 'guided democracy' – set in place by Birendra's father Mahendra – found it had to rise to the occasion. Political parties were immediately hijacked by wheeler-dealers and lost their ideological moorings. As lack of imagination at the top became clear, opportunistic politicians of the extreme left decided to take a short-cut to power by spouting Maoism and brandishing the gun. To their surprise, they found undereducated, hopeless youths answering their call. Starting from the midhills of western Nepal, the Maoists spread like brushfire and sucked the energy from the democratic process.

The royal massacre, carried out by a disenchanted crown prince with ready access to automatic weaponry, took away from the scene a personality who had tried to play by the rules of the new game, a figure who had been a constant presence before the citizens for nearly 30 years, 20 as absolute king and

11 as constitutional monarch. As importantly, it severely weakened an institution that needs to stand steadfastly behind Nepal's parliamentary democracy, at a time when it is still finding its feet. Nepal can ill afford this: the monarchy is not indispensable for the people to remain Nepalis – but it made the decisive dynastic contribution to the creation of a Nepali state, remains one of few unifying factors in a country of enormous geographical and demographic diversity, has a deep-rooted social and cultural role to play, and has an enormous economic contribution to make in a country overwhelmingly reliant on tourism.

King Prithvinarayan Shah was the ruler of the small, central Nepalese principality of Gorkha, one of over two dozen interminably warring satraps that at the beginning of the eighteenth century ruled parcels of the central Himalayan chain. Prithvinarayan devised a system of conquest and consolidation that brought these hill principalities under the House of Gorkha, and his biggest prize was the conquest of Kathmandu Valley in 1768, to where he shifted his capital. The expansionary wars were continued by his descendants until they were forced to desist by the British, who through a treaty in 1816 truncated Nepal to its present size.

Rather than join Nepal to their expanding empire, the British preferred to let the Kathmandu court rule over its territory as long as it showed fealty to the East India Company, and subsequently the British government. Thus kept from expanding its geographic control, the court in Kathmandu became a hive of intrigues, and during one such violent episode the monarchy was sidelined and a system of hereditary prime ministers was introduced. Nepal became a shogunate under the Ranas, who ruled absolutely for 104 years, until King Tribhuvan overthrew the oligarchy.

Tribhuvan's son, King Mahendra, conducted a royal takeover in 1960, shoving aside the elected government of the day and jailing his democrat opponents. He devised the Panchayat system, a kind of guided democracy which provided a multi-tiered system of representation but was commanded in all essential aspects by Mahendra himself. Mahendra pushed Nepal into the modern era through a process of infrastructure building, social and economic development, and the creation of a nationalist ideology. A core group of Nepalis who had been socialised in British India continues to provide the momentum for the Nepali state today.

Mahendra's son Birendra, educated in Darjeeling and overseas, took over in 1971. Birendra was a well-meaning but ineffective monarch: an attempt to modernise education was still-born, the bureaucracy became bloated, and foreign policy was allowed to stagnate. When the people reacted against the authoritarian nature of the system in 1979–80, King Birendra called a plebiscite, asking the people whether they wanted a multiparty democracy or an 'improved' (how, was not specified) Panchayat system. The latter won with a small margin, and Birendra got to rule as an absolute monarch for another decade; at which point, as a democratic wave engulfed Eastern Europe and the Soviet Union, political agitation returned. The People's Movement of spring 1990 was not a revolution, but an uprising of the urban middle classes. To his credit, King Birendra did not wait for the bloodshed to escalate, and called for a multiparty democracy and a new constitution.

### Birendra's constitutional monarchy

The 1990 constitution, written by nominees of the main political parties and the royal palace, firmly established Nepal as a parliamentary democracy and constitutional monarchy. The demands of the new system, where the king reigns rather than rules and follows the dictates of the elected prime minister, seemed to suit the personality of King Birendra perfectly. The King's responsibilities quickly dwindled to acting as ceremonial head of state, reading out the government's message to parliament, and carrying out religious and cultural activities demanded of him.

Birendra, with the rest of the public, watched the politicians and political parties quickly misuse the trust reposed in them to exploit the system for personal gain. Over time, with the King performing his role as constitutional monarch and the political parties beginning to understand the system, there might have been a proper evolution. But then the Maoists intervened, taking advantage of public disenchantment.

As the Maoists began to spread, and it became clear that the civilian police was not equipped to deal with an insurgency, it became necessary to involve the Royal Nepal Army. The military, however, has traditionally been led by men from the 'Thakuri' clans, descendants of the fighting elite of earlier times, who consider themselves close to royalty. The generals retained loyalty to the king as 'supreme commander-in-chief'.

Under the constitution of 1990, the army has to function under the directives of a National Security Council, in which members of the civilian government have a majority over the army. However, the top brass refused to go into action even when the civilian government asked it to. King Birendra's one act of political involvement as constitutional monarch may have been to refuse to let the military engage the Maoists at a time when it would have been relatively easy.

King Birendra would have been watching the movement of the burgeoning Maoists across the midhills with increasing concern when disaster struck from a different direction on 1 June 2001. A possibly drunk Crown Prince, said to be distraught over his parents' refusal to allow him to marry the lady of his choice, burst into a family reception with several automatic weapons. King Birendra died with the words, 'What have you gone and done?' on his lips. Of the 24 people in the room, only nine survived, and those who died included Queen Aishwarya, Birendra's brother Dhirendra, sister Shanti, daughter Shruti and son Nirajan.

The devastation was so great that the survival of the family of the remaining brother Gyanendra resulted in paroxysms of conspiracy-seeking on the streets of Kathmandu, fuelled by the Maoists and others who viewed the royalty as unequivocally feudal. But there was nothing for the Royal Commission to do but to crown the 54-year-old Gyanendra as king as the only survivor of the royal carnage.

### Gyanendra on the throne

While his brother had become king, Gyanendra had concentrated on making money, running a corporate house with wide-ranging interests, and dabbling in contracts and commissions. He also headed a conservation effort named after his father, a trust which has been actively seeking to preserve ecological diversity and promote environmentally sensitive development. However, nothing would have prepared anyone to become the king under such trying circumstances. The fact that the public was unwilling to accept that the Crown Prince was a mass murderer became a handicap for Gyanendra, who could do little to make the people believe that the crown had been thrust on him.

The sheer scale of the Narayanhiti tragedy and the 'unbelievability factor' kept the Nepali populace even from properly mourning the mass deaths in the royal palace. Gyanendra has no choice but to let time heal the wounds, while carrying out the responsibilities of the Nepali king, both according to the ancient ritualistic dictates – such as paying obeisance to Kumari, the virgin goddess of Kathmandu – and according to formal requirements as head of state. However, as a country in severe and multiple crisis, Nepal requires a king who can also guide the people in tackling the vicissitudes of modernisation, economic globalisation and the invasion of Western cultural mores. It is clear that King Gyanendra has the personality to attempt these grave challenges, but only time will bring a change to the public's attitude towards his monarchy.

### Need for a Nepali kingship

Unlike some kings of the modern era in Europe and Asia, whose kingships are non-traditional implants, the Nepali monarchy has been part and parcel of Nepal's history. Can such a traditional kingship make adjustments into the modern era? Birendra's largely correct, decade-long performance as constitutional monarch has set a political precedent for his younger brother to follow. But Nepal's sizeable social, economic and cultural challenges may require a more active approach. Nepal possesses one of the worst education and public health systems in the world. Unlike countries that were colonised, Nepal entered the modern era immediately and without preparation, creating enormous dislocations that have been fed by the arrival of satellite television, a highways network, and consumer goods. Traditional values have been swiftly overtaken, while modern-day values have not been introduced to take their place. The demographic diversity of the country – it has 23 million people, at least 40 languages and hundreds of discrete ethnic groups and communities – makes this transition all the more difficult, for traditional lifestyles and cultures are disappearing before they have even been properly understood by ethnographers. Without doubt, the institution of kingship is of great use to the country and people, as a symbol of continuity, of national unity, and as a guide in the transition to modernity.

The propaganda machine of the Panchayat era tried to convince the people that the Nepali monarchy – one which ruled as well as reigned – was essential for the survival of the Nepali nation-state in the Central Himalaya. The transition into democracy disproved that claim. But kingship, the Nepali kingship, is seen rightly or wrongly by the majority of Nepalis as the institution of 'last resort' if the country really goes into a tailspin. That was one additional reason why the death and departure of King Birendra meant so much for the people in far-flung communities.

King Gyanendra starts his duties with multiple handicaps, including the distrust of much of the public, the suspicion of the political parties, and a Maoist insurgency. A constitutional monarch should be seen to be apolitical, but this is difficult in such a volatile situation. The trick lies in building trust between the new king and the political parties. The new man on the serpent-backed throne needs to understand that any behind-the-scenes political activity should be solely to support multiparty parliamentary democracy.

The unrepresentative Panchayat system left Nepal as an underdeveloped country in the twenty-first century, and 12 years of democracy since 1990 had begun to stimulate media freedom, decentralisation, and peaceful party politics, before the Maoist insurgency put everything on hold.

Meanwhile, there is the Maoist demand for a 'republic', keeping in mind that many progressives in the mainstream parties see kingship as an obsolete artefact of a feudal era. Would that modernisation came so easily!

*Kanak Mani Dixit is a Nepal-based journalist and editor of the South Asian magazine* Himal.